Spectacular Bodies, Dangerous Borders: Three New Latin American Plays

PATRICIA SUÁREZ
Matchmaker

LUIS ENRIQUE GUTIÉRREZ ORTIZ MONASTERIO
The Girls from the 3.5 Floppies

GUSTAVO OTT
Passport

Edited by
ANA ELENA PUGA

Translated by Ana Elena Puga and Heather L. McKay

LATR Books
University of Kansas
Colección Antología Margaret Sayers Peden No. 1

Puga, Ana Elena, ed.
   Spectacular Bodies, Dangerous Borders: Three New Latin American Plays. Lawrence,
KS: LATR Books, 2011. [Patricia Suárez, *Matchmaker*; Luis Enrique Gutiérrez Ortiz
Monasterio, *The Girls from the 3.5 Floppies*; Gustavo Ott, *Passport*] Edited by Ana
Elena Puga, with translations by Ana Elena Puga and Heather L. McKay [Colección
Antología Margaret Sayers Peden No. 1].

ISBN 978-1-4507-7876-3

LATR Books
Spanish and Portuguese
University of Kansas
Lawrence, Kansas 66045
Email: day@ku.edu
www.latrbooks.org
Series Editor: Sarah M. Misemer
Managing Editor: Stuart A. Day
Editorial Assistants: Katya Soll, Regan Postma

First printing, June 2011

Design and typesetting:
Pam LeRow, Digital Media Services
College of Liberal Arts and Sciences
University of Kansas

Printed in the US by:
Allen Press, Inc.
Lawrence, KS 66044

This series is made possible through a generous grant from the
College of Liberal Arts and Sciences of the University of Kansas.

Contents

Dedicated to the memory of George Woodyard

Acknowledgments

We wish to thank the playwrights, Patricia Suárez, Luis Enrique Gutiérrez Ortiz Monasterio (LEGOM), and Gustavo Ott, for their collaboration with this project. LATR Books editors Sarah M. Misemer and Stuart A. Day have been supportive and patient throughout the process, providing guidance that improved the introduction and the translations. Finally, the former series editor of LATR Books, the late George Woodyard, nurtured the formation of this volume as he nurtured many other scholarly endeavors in the field of Latin American theater for more than four decades until his death on November 7, 2010. The volume is therefore dedicated to his memory.

Spectacular Bodies, Dangerous Borders

The three contemporary Latin American plays in this volume deploy different aesthetic styles and hail from widely divergent countries of origin – Argentina, Mexico, and Venezuela – yet they all stage bodies under assault from international markets that trade flesh and bone as just another commodity. In these works, female bodies, male bodies, virgin bodies, sex-worker bodies, domestic bodies, and immigrant bodies suffer violence on the material or metaphoric borders between nations. Because it is set in 1920, in a Polish village that exports its impoverished young Jewish women to Buenos Aires brothels, Patricia Suárez's *Matchmaker* [*Casamentera*] reminds us that the international trade in women's bodies is not just a late twentieth or twenty-first-century phenomenon. For the two sex-worker mothers in *The Girls from the 3.5 Floppies* [*Las chicas del tres y media floppies*], by Luis Enrique Gutiérrez Ortiz Monasterio (LEGOM), the sale of their bodies is part of the struggle to survive daily life in a Mexican borderland marked by violence, drug addiction, and lack of economic opportunity.[1] And in *Passport*, set in an unidentified railway station anywhere in the world, Venezuelan dramatist Gustavo Ott creates a protagonist caught up in a whirlwind of physical assaults that brings to mind the post-9/11 insanity of places as disparate as Guantanamo, Abu Ghraib, or O'Hare Airport. For these characters, everything from a routine attempt to pass through a train station checkpoint to an arranged marriage requiring transatlantic migration becomes a life-threatening experience. Under these circumstances, the body becomes spectacular in the sense that it attracts attention and becomes the center of a variety of performances: some self-generated and others created, not just by the voyeuristic gaze but also by acts of physical violence.

These plays also highlight how spectacular bodies marked by gender and/or ethnicity are often subject to danger during attempts to cross national, legal, or other boundaries. As Ramón H. Rivera-Servera and Harvey Young argue, borders do not merely delineate geographical limits but, by creating barriers that challenge

---

[1] I prefer to use the term "sex work" rather than "prostitution" when referring to contemporary women in order to avoid the moral stigma attached to the latter term; I will continue to use the term "prostitution" to discuss the historical, legal, and archetypal frameworks in which these portrayals of contemporary sex workers must operate.

would-be crossers to find a way through, over, under, or around them, they also function as agents in the process of motion required by crossings (2). During these crossings, borders can become dangerous sites in which bodies undergo scrutiny, both the Foucauldian biopolitical scrutiny of the State in surveillance mode, controlling the political subject, and the less official but equally fraught scrutiny of the private entrepreneur in a globalized economy assessing, protecting, and exploiting the value of his/her human cargo. For gendered bodies marked by surveillance and the law, as Peggy Phelan has noted, visibility is a trap (6-7). Once trapped, in a metaphorical sense, the spectacular body itself can become a dangerous border that incarnates the contradictions of a world in which goods are increasingly free to circulate while the motion of human beings is increasingly restricted. From their respective perspectives, all three playwrights create characters who assume the risks associated with border crossings, not as valiant attempts to resist such a world but as simple efforts to survive.

There Are No Victims Here

In both Suárez's and LEGOM's plays, the experience of women who engage in sex work is represented in unromantic and unsentimental terms. These protagonists have little in common, say, with either Gabriel García Márquez's tender Eréndira or with Roberto Bolaño's murderous *puta*, not to mention the whores played for laughs in Mario Vargas Llosa's *Pantaleón y las visitadoras*. The prostitute with a heart of gold familiar from so many works of Latin American film and literature is also conspicuously absent.[2] Instead, both LEGOM and Suárez eschew melodrama and victimization of their protagonists. While their works sometimes provoke laughter, it is a laughter laced with compassion for hapless characters trying to make the best of terrible situations: LEGOM's bawdy sense of humor jolts the spectator into recognition of human folly; Suárez's more gentle Chekhovian wit has a slower pace but just as long a rapier.

Born in Rosario, Argentina in 1969, Suárez is the youngest of these three playwrights, all of whom are still under fifty. She studied first psychology and then anthropology at the National University in Rosario before dropping out to devote herself to writing fiction. Known as much for her novels, short stories, and children's books as for her theater, she burst onto the Buenos Aires theatrical

---

[2] For in-depth studies of the figure of the prostitute in Latin American literature, see Castillo and Solomon. For a fine study that focuses on the prostitute in literature and film, see de la Mora.

scene with the trilogy *The Polish Women* [*Las polacas*] in 2002, which she wrote after studying with the playwright Mauricio Kartun. *Matchmaker* [*Casamentera*] is the second play in the trilogy. In 2005, Suárez enjoyed at least four different productions of her plays in Buenos Aires.[3] Since then, she has increasingly collaborated with others, such as Leonel Giacometto and María Rosa Pfeiffer, yet has also continued to write individually. More recent works include *The Mystic Rose* [*La rosa mística*, 2009], directed by Gustavo Ott in Caracas, and *Shots Fired for Love* [*Disparos por amor*, 2010], directed by Jorge Cassino in Madrid. While her plays have been produced in Venezuela and Spain, this is the first published English translation of her drama. As of this writing, however, a musical version of *The Polish Women* is scheduled for 2012 under the direction of Hugo Medrano at GALA Hispanic Theatre in Washington, DC.

In an introduction to the Spanish-language edition of *The Polish Women*, Kartun notes that the dramatic trilogy powerfully evokes Argentina without ever directly staging that country. The action of the first play takes place on a train crossing the Polish border (*Tartar Stories/Historias tártaras*); the second is set in a living room somewhere in rural Poland (*Matchmaker/Casamentera*); and the third unfolds on a boat in mid-ocean on its way back to Buenos Aires (*The Warsaw Club/La Varsovia*). Building on Kartun's insight, Sharon Magnarelli persuasively argues that the off-stage spaces "allude to the illusions not only of theater itself but also to those of sociopolitical reality, illusions that in both cases are created and manipulated by the powerful who always remain just out of site and sight" (38). I would add that *Matchmaker* also shows how the supposedly powerless can also create and manipulate illusions, blurring the line between passivity and agency. The creation of illusion in the service of resistance, or game-playing, as Jacqueline Bixler and Catherine Larson have called it, gives the female characters in *Matchmaker* a measure of control over their destiny and renders them far more complex than the usual suffering melodrama victims. The construction of liminal spaces occupied by characters that dwell in the gray zones between good and evil makes the play a model of subtle, delicate craftsmanship. Magnarelli notes that the victims' survival "depends on their exploitation of some of the same tricks of illusion (theater) that the victimizers employ, in what lends an impressive depth and complexity to both the sociohistorical events themselves and to the plays, as it suggests that the women, while unquestionably victims here, are not all totally disempowered" (41). I would go further: the lines between victim and victimizer are so blurred that what Elizabeth M. Schneider calls the "false dichotomy of victimization and agency" is almost completely deconstructed (1). Suárez helps us to imagine a world in which the "injured prostitute" transcends the role of suffering female victim awaiting rescue.[4]

To tweak the title of Hillary Clinton's book *It Takes a Village*, *Matchmaker* shows how, in a globalized world of ever-tightening economic networks, it takes a village to produce a prostitute. The character of the matchmaker, Mrs. Golde, uses a photo of her beautiful daughter Ada as bait for Schlomo, a pimp posing as an innocent suitor in search of an arranged marriage, supposedly looking for a bride to take back to Buenos Aires. Once Schlomo shows interest, however, Mrs. Golde puts into motion an elaborate bait-and-switch routine in which Ada, going under the assumed name of "Edit," feigns mental disability so that Schlomo will lose interest and eventually agree to pay more money for a less physically attractive village girl, Emma, who is not an "idiot." Mrs. Golde never reveals to Schlomo that Edit/Ada is in fact her daughter, passing her off instead as Emma's sister. Emma's father, it turns out, is most likely aware that his daughter is being sold into prostitution under the false pretense of an arranged marriage. Even Emma herself cooperates in the deception, given her family's desperate economic situation and fed by the hope, perhaps also an illusion, that once in Buenos Aires she can get help from a Jewish aid society to escape the fate of imprisonment in a brothel. This is far from the treacly theatrical universe of that other Jewish matchmaker play *Fiddler on the Roof*.

Matchmaker, like the other two plays in the trilogy, is loosely based on the historical facts of a forced-prostitution trade in European women in late nineteenth and early twentieth-century Argentina. While the majority of sex workers in Buenos Aires were neither Jewish nor from Eastern Europe and not all of the sex work was forced, a significant portion of the market in "white slaves" was cornered by Jewish pimps. These men organized into associations such as La Varsovia, formed in 1907 and re-organized under the name Zwi Migdal in 1927, as part of an unsuccessful attempt to avoid criminal prosecution (Guy 122). Because mainstream Jewish society ostracized denizens of the sex-work underworld, the associations facilitated socializing, business life, and even religious observance, primarily through the purchase of land to establish synagogues and cemeteries.

---

[4] See Doezema for the argument that some contemporary attempts to rescue trafficking victims serve the interests of First-World feminists more than those of the Third-World sex workers they ostensibly want to help.

As depicted in *Matchmaker*, Jewish pimps would sometimes participate in false religious marriages, taking advantage of strict traditions mandating a wife's submission to her husband to pressure their "wives" to cooperate with their plans to prostitute them (Guy 8-9.) Prostitution was legal in Argentina between 1875 and 1936; forced prostitution was not. Yet police were often paid off to look the other way and could not be counted upon to help women who tried to escape brothels. In the famous case of Raquel Lieberman, however, criminal charges were finally brought against the Zwi Migdal organization and its leader Luis Zwi Migdal in 1930, after Lieberman testified that her husband and the organization had forced her back into prostitution years after she had left the profession to open an antique shop (Guy 129). While more than a hundred men were initially arrested in a round-up following Lieberman's denunciation, in the end all but three were released and a handful were deported (Guy 129; Vincent 185-86).

The character of Mrs. Golde reminds us that women in the Argentine skin trade were not simply passive victims of male pimps: they were often active as procurers of other women and as madams of brothels. Far from being a victim, Mrs. Golde organizes the sale of Emma to economically support her daughter and her grandchild, the daughter's out-of-wedlock baby, which Mrs. Golde passes off as her own son. The seductive phrasing of Mrs. Golde's appeal to Emma for noble self-sacrifice avoids the sort of explicit threats a crudely crafted villain might have issued and instead employs the combination of kindness, euphemism, and apparent sincerity common to the rationalization of moral economies that promote the self-sacrifice of poor young women around the world today, from Filipino domestic workers exported to wealthier parts of Asia to undocumented Central American women working as maids in the United States: "If everything goes wrong, we will be by your side in our hearts. It won't last more than three years, then they'll let you go. It won't last forever. You've climbed out of poverty; you will help your own. Isn't that what matters?" (49).[5] Focused on taking care of

---

[5] See Ong for an analysis of the moral economy of female migrant workers in Asia. According to the US State Department's *Trafficking in Persons Report 2010*, sex workers in Argentina today are most often from Paraguay, Brazil, Peru, and the Dominican Republic. The report also maintains that most Eastern European women and children forced into sex work are smuggled into other parts of Europe. In the United States, according to the report, most of the victims of sex trafficking are US citizens, while most of the victims of labor trafficking are foreigners (338). A controversial *New York Times Magazine* article published in 2004, "The Girls Next Door," by Peter Landesman, however, has helped create the impression that sex trafficking of Eastern European women is widespread in the United States and

her own kin, at the expense of other village girls who face a dismal fate whether at home or abroad, Mrs. Golde is the middle manager, neither the powerful nor the powerless. Her metatheatrical conniving – like a theatrical director, she assigns the roles to her daughter and the other village girls – protects a privileged minority at the expense of an exploited majority.

Under her mother's direction, Edit/Ada uses an apparent lack of physical control of her own body as an actual exercise in masterful physical self-control, acting, in the theatrical sense, in order to help determine a favorable outcome in a dangerous situation. Playing the "idiot," she limits herself to a one-word script ("Bathroom!") and a single bodily function, urination, at the precise moment necessary to interrupt Schlomo's attempt to kiss Emma. In her case, visibility is a trap set for another, namely Schlomo. Hers is a spectacular body in dissent that uses a creative resistance strategy akin to that of some characters analyzed by Daphne A. Brooks. While Brooks's discussion of African-American slave characters who feign stupidity in order to "destabilize the subjectivity of the ruling class" pertains to a very different time and place, namely the antebellum United States, it nevertheless illuminates the parallel form of subterfuge undertaken by Edit/Ada during her game-playing (1-13). Feigning mental disability and physical lack of self-control paradoxically becomes Edit/Ada's route to freedom from being forced into sex work. Drooling and sucking her thumb are her version of the minstrel "puttin on ole massa" in order to escape enslavement (Brooks 2).

The most obvious potential victim in *Matchmaker* is Emma, the young woman who agrees to leave Poland to go off to Buenos Aires with Schlomo in a marriage that will likely turn out to be false. Yet even Emma is not entirely powerless: she has a plan for seeking help, devised with the help of Mrs. Golde, and she displays a lively intelligence that will most likely serve her well in Buenos Aires. She also has the advantage of going into the bargain with Schlomo with her eyes wide open as to the nature of his trade, a knowledge she carefully keeps from him. Perhaps by coincidence, "Emma" was the name of a famous Buenos Aires madam of the era who became wealthy and boasted a legendary collection of jewelry (Guy 127-28). One could imagine the charming Emma, if she does not escape her fate, becoming the millionaire madam.

Schlomo could easily be construed as the villain of the play. At one point he threatens to kill Golde, breaking the drawing-room politeness of most of the

Mexico, particularly after the article was adapted into the popular film *Trade*, written by José Rivera (dir. Marco Kreuzpaintner, 2007). The trope of the Eastern European sex "slave" has since been further popularized by various television shows.

dialogue to reveal the underworld of violence in which he operates. Yet Suárez leaves open the remote possibility that he really is in love with Emma and will not sell her as he has sold others. This detail distances him from the tradition of mustache-twirlers who tie the heroine to the railroad tracks. And of course, the dubious last-minute conversion of a pimp-turned-suitor who has made a career of selling young women into brothels hardly constitutes a melodramatic redemption for Schlomo or a fairy-tale happy ending for Emma. Schlomo's attempt to play the role of suitor reads instead as yet another instance of metatheatrical irony.

An important consideration for staging is the metaphoric superimposition of two countries, Poland and Argentina, in a single location: Mrs. Golde's parlor in rural Poland. For instance, in one scene, the girls ponder the strange Argentine slang (*Lunfardo*) for various words, bringing Argentina into the room and yet alienating, in the Brechtian sense of making the familiar strange, expressions that an Argentine audience member might use every day. Argentine spectators would find the scene humorous because it gives them a glimpse of themselves as seen from the outside, even by other Latin Americans, since *Lunfardo* is limited to Argentine usage. For a non-Argentine audience outside of both Latin America and Poland, however, the scene might become more about the hybridization of two unfamiliar cultures. The humor then derives from recognition of the misunderstandings that arise when crossing cultural as well as geographical national borders.

Working Mothers, No Need for Rescue

Reviewers of *The Girls from the 3.5 Floppies* [*Las chicas del tres y media floppies*] have sometimes described the play as if it were a sentimental tragedy about two good women forced into prostitution for the sake of nurturing their children. Such interpretations miss the genius of LEGOM, which is that his characters are hard-as-nails without being wooden, unrealistic yet extremely human, endowed with the hyper-humanity mysteriously conjured by puppets, cartoons, and other animated figures. Other reviewers have described LEGOM's work as cynical, yet that also misses the mark, because no matter how exaggeratedly obscene or ridiculous the characters may seem, we feel something for them. What we feel, however, is not necessarily always pity; instead sometimes we feel awe at the massive grotesqueness of their actions. Despite a paucity of character names, in LEGOM's theater the emphasis is always on character, in part because his plays include no stage directions. Action, ideas, spectacle, and character psychology are all relayed through razor-sharp dialogue that makes the macho language of US playwrights such as Sam Shepard and David Mamet seem tame by comparison.

Born in Guadalajara, Mexico in 1968, LEGOM has made his home in Querétaro and Veracruz, where he serves as resident playwright for the Universidad Veracruzana's theater company. Besides *The Girls from the 3.5 Floppies*, his major plays include *Queer Sensation* [*Sensacional de maricones*, 2005], *About Beasts, Creatures, and Dogs* [*De bestias, criaturas y perras*, 2003], *I Hate the Fucking Mexicans* [*Odio a los putos mexicanos*, 2006], and *Civilization* [*Civilización*, 2007]. His plays have been translated into French, Italian, and English. *Girls* (as I will refer to *The Girls from the 3.5 Floppies*) premiered at the theater festival DramaFest in Mexico City in 2004 in a Spanish-language production directed by the National Theatre of Scotland's John Tiffany. The play soon acquired an international life as it travelled to Edinburgh's Fringe Festival the following year, where it won a Fringe First award. In 2008, Tiffany's production toured the US, with productions in Denver, Chicago, and Atlanta. When I saw the production at Chicago's Museum of Contemporary Art, I was stunned by how well the fast-paced direction and precise comic timing of the actors, Aída López and Gabriela Murray, made the dialogue's acid wit sizzle.

In *Girls*, a series of snappy one-liners quickly reveals that the two nameless female characters use sex work both to help pay their children's school fees and to feed their cocaine habits. Although it seems one character considers herself superior and appears to be in control as she constantly puts down her more naïve friend with a steady stream of mildly obscene insults, both, in fact, have extremely limited room in which to exercise agency. Their choices, as LEGOM colorfully enumerates them in a program note from the 2008 US tour, are: "Pay little Joaquín's school fees or blow the lot on coke and go clubbing to the 3.5 Floppies? Clean the apartment so your estranged kids can visit or let your penniless pal move back in and risk everything? And what about the irresistible offer from the men in Tijuana?" The mysterious men in Tijuana, we learn from the naïve friend, have literally ripped the face off of someone who fell afoul of them. Yet just as the impoverished Eastern European girls in *Matchmaker* perceive few alternatives for themselves and are inexorably drawn to the glamour of 1920s Buenos Aires, the "girls" who hook at the cyber-themed 3.5 Floppies bar in Mexico today are inevitably attracted to the money and the drug thugs on the US border.

The border in *Girls* is just up the highway, not across an ocean, yet the world of the "gringos" that intersects and overlaps with the Mexican women's world is in many ways as inscrutable to them as *Lunfardo* appears to the Polish girls. The more naïve of the two women regularly watches *Sponge Bob* in her clients'

clients' hotel rooms but after five years, all the English she can muster, her only slightly more sophisticated friend teases her, is "tu foquen dic, machote" (66). When the so-called developed and developing worlds intersect, the women inevitably lose, yet the two worlds are inextricably linked; the spectacle of their commodified, gendered bodies is all the women have to offer in a global marketplace. Violent Mexican narcos, Japanese sex tourists, wealthy Arabs, and gringo clients are the buyers; the women have only their bodies to sell. In a world of Internet and instant global communication, the irony is that the women are almost completely isolated: they have no supportive family or friends, no numbers in their phonebooks, and no one to call for help despite their access to free long-distance.

Sergio de la Mora has argued insightfully that Mexico's national-origin narratives include not only mothers, but also prostitutes and prostitutes who are also mothers. According to de la Mora, in the post-revolutionary period, the prostitute motif embodies altered gender relations and social identities: "The prostitute is also an allegory for the exploitation and feminization of the labor force" (33). In an era of globalization's dangerous borders, I would argue, LEGOM recycles the prostitute as an allegorical figure for a feminized work force, yet simultaneously deploys parody and farce to explode two intersecting stereotypes at the core of the Mexican national imaginary—the suffering, self-abnegating mother and the saintly sex worker.[6] Combining de la Mora's insights with those of Jo Doezema on the essential conservatism of the impulse to rescue sex workers, I would also argue that LEGOM rejects the morality of melodrama and exposes the impulse to save anyone, even oneself, as ludicrous. And yet *Girls* is not a play that shrugs its shoulders at poverty and violence or blames the women themselves for their own exploitation. On the contrary, LEGOM performs the radical act of suggesting that these characters are not victims, that they do not require empathy, sympathy, or rescue, but that there is nevertheless something terribly wrong with the world that ultimately destroys them. Globalized and neoliberalized Mexico, in this scenario, becomes a realm in which women's bodies become spectacular sites of violence and Mexican men (except for drug traffickers) are mostly powerless and irrelevant.

Both of *Girls'* protagonists are comically less-than-sterling examples of idealized motherhood. One woman has long ago given up custody of her children

---

[6] See de la Mora and Castillo for valuable analyses of how the figure of the saintly sex worker was immortalized in Federico Gamboa's 1903 novel *Santa* (Castillo 37-62; de la Mora 31-42).

to her ex and shows little interest in them at all; the second thinks of her son mainly as a burden. Instead of sacrificing for him, she wants to use the money for his school fees to buy cocaine. All this is depicted without moral judgment and without encouragement to would-be rescuers in the audience, who are kept firmly at bay by the matter-of-fact vulgarity of the nameless female characters:

> You haven't seen your kids?
>
> What do you want me to see in them?
>
> I don't know, whatever mothers see in them. The eyes, for instance. Some check out their backside, others pay a lot of attention to their hairstyle. I don't know.
>
> Well not me. Did they tell you that the Arabs are going to give a wet t-shirt party? (74-75)

The character who demonstrates concern about the other woman's children hands over her own child to his grandparents and shows little interest in investigating the possibility that her own mother may have died. Even the characters' occasional yearning for a more conventional life becomes fodder for black humor. The woman who has given up custody of her kids cleans almost continuously throughout the first scene (in John Tiffany's production, actor Aída López mopped the floor with frenetic energy), leading her friend to comment: "You want to learn to be a homemaker mom and all that stuff" (69). The first woman vehemently denies the charge. There will be no redemptions, no conversions, and no family reunions for these women.

And yet the Virgin Mary and a box full of Bibles play a significant role in the drama, if only as a source of further parody. One woman keeps her cocaine hidden inside a statue of the Virgin of Fátima. The other steals Bibles from her clients' hotel rooms but never bothers to read them, imagining that they are some sort of serial in which each volume is different. She views the Bibles as her "insurance," thinking that one day she might be able to sell them, a fantasy that parallels how some semi-believers practice religion as a social ritual, as "insurance" in case it turns out that there is in fact a God who will meet us in the afterlife (77). But in the end, the Bibles prove useless and the women conclude that their existence is worth "pure fucking dick" (87). In perhaps the only moment in which the play indulges in genuine emotion without parody, love is expressed in purely secular terms. "Have I told you that I love you?" one woman asks the other (88). The sentimental reply would be, "I love you too." But instead the other character replies, "Yes, many times, many times" (88). Then the subject quickly changes. In LEGOM's theatrical universe, God exists only as a joke or as a conspicuous absence, not as a source of love or comfort.

The spectacle of suffering bodies in *Girls* is never depicted on stage; instead its goriness is described in comic grotesqueness or suggested indirectly. Suffering does not circulate in what I have elsewhere called the "political economy of suffering," in which bodily pain is commodified and exchanged for spectator sympathy.[7] Instead, the unglamorous commodification of the women's bodies – underscored in Tiffany's production by costumes (Bertha Romero) that revealed belly fat protruding from below halter tops – itself becomes a dangerous border, a border between "normal" working-class life and underworld violence. For these liminal bodies, as we learn from the characters' monologues, to be seen poses extreme danger: vaginas are slashed or serve as receptacles for snakes during sex shows; a woman drowns as a boat full of Japanese sex tourists applauds. And bodies are described, in equally gruesome metatheatrical moments, as making "ferocious noises" during the performances required by sex work, performances which are mocked and exposed as farcical (69). Yet for all the parody of spectacle, being seen and heard remains dangerous for these characters: their bodies are not the explicit bodies of performance artists in dissent against masculinized desire and their own commodification as objects of desire.[8] Thus, when we spectators position ourselves in this scenario, if we are not permitted to imagine ourselves as rescuers, neither are we encouraged to view ourselves as admirers. Perhaps we are voyeurs, or even potential meal tickets.

To Look or Not to Look

In *Passport*, Ott vividly depicts the body as spectacle and dangerous border through its protagonist, Eugene, a hapless traveler in a train station who hands over his passport to a soldier, who in turn promptly disappears with it. The soldier soon returns, however, accompanied by an officer, in order to interrogate and physically abuse the traveler – for not having a passport. Things quickly go from bad to worse for Eugene, recalling the horrors suffered by so many characters in so many works by playwrights who specialize in the absurdity of

---

[7] See "Poor Enrique and Poor María, Or the Political Economy of Suffering in Two Migrant Melodramas" for my analysis of how suffering is traded in performances by and about migrants in the journalistic account *Enrique's Journey*, by Sonia Nazario, and in the documentary film *De Nadie*, by Tín Dirdamal.

[8] See Hart's anthology for a wide variety of essays analyzing the spectacle of women's bodies in contemporary theater; see Schneider for a study of contemporary female performance artists and their strategies for resisting commodification.

modern bureaucracy and its indulgence in abusive power, from Eugène Ionesco to Harold Pinter to Griselda Gambaro. Yet Ott's play is distinguished by how its action and visual imagery bring to mind our post-9/11 world, with its US-perpetrated torture and its intense surveillance justified by threats of terrorism, real and imagined. If Suárez's and LEGOM's works feature bodies in motion between departures and arrivals, Ott's *Passport* confronts us with a body in stasis, detained between its place of origin and its destination. If Suárez and LEGOM denied us direct ocular access to the brutalities they reference – no peeks into the brothel or on-stage violence against women – Ott asks us to train our gaze on theatrical versions of disturbing images made all too familiar by our own news media. Whereas *Matchmaker* and *Girls* refuse the traditional trope of victim, *Passport* revisits it, but with a difference.

Born in Caracas, Venezuela in 1963, Ott has written more than two dozen plays, founded a major theater company, Teatro San Martín de Caracas, and established himself as a significant presence on the international theater circuit in Europe and Latin America. His works have been translated into many languages, including English, many by Heather L. McKay, who translated the version of *Passport* included here. Ott is regularly staged by GALA Hispanic Theatre in Washington, DC, which under the direction of Abel López produced *Divorcées, Evangelicals, and Vegetarians* [*Divorciadas, evangélicas y vegetarianas*], which premiered in 2003 and was revived in 2011. López also directed *Molotov Kisses* [*Tu ternura Molotov*, 2008], *I Never Said I was a Good Girl* [*Nunca dije que era una niña buena*, 1997], and *Pavlov: Two Seconds Before the Crime* [*Pavlov: dos segundos antes del crimen*, 1995]. In 2009, GALA staged *Momia en el closet: The Return of Eva Perón*, for which Ott wrote the lyrics, directed by Mariano Caligaris. In 2002, New York's Public Theater produced a staged reading of *80 Teeth, 4 Feet, and 500 Pounds* [*80 dientes, 4 metros y 200 kilos*] and the following year staged a reading of *Two Loves and a Creature* [*Dos amores y un bicho*]. *Passport* premiered in Madrid (1991) and has toured Latin America, but has not yet been fully produced in the United States. A bilingual staged reading, however, was directed by Arlene Martinez-Vickers in a 2011 co-production by Seattle's eSe Teatro and the Central Heating Lab at A Contemporary Theatre. Whether in essentially serious dramas like *80 Teeth*, which deals with sexual assault and guilt in its aftermath, or in lighter comedies like *Divorcées*, a celebration of the redemptive power of friendship, and *Molotov Kisses*, a romantic comedy with a terrorist twist, Ott displays a dark sense of humor that is wonderfully playful yet returns obsessively to violence. His characters' language is often brisk, almost matter-of-fact, yet it can be suddenly interrupted by surrealist imagery and poetic riffs that invite meditation on ongoing horrors.

As John Torpey elucidates in *The Invention of the Passport: Surveillance, Citizenship and the State*, nation-states use passports and other identity documents to make us "legible" to them, in the word preferred by political scientist James C. Scott, or to "embrace us" in their legal arms, to use Torpey's preferred metaphor for the demarcation of members versus intruders (2-20). Ott's play, however, in part because of its setting in an anonymous railway station anywhere in the world, shows how such documents not only prop up state authority but also help create extra-official zones in which freelancers can carry out intimidation or even torture, which may or may not be engineered by the state. Eugene's tormenters, the anonymous Soldier and Officer, may or may not be following orders. This pair of torturers, by contrast to, say, the pair of dumb waiters at the beck and call of a dumbwaiter in Harold Pinter's play by the same name or the two thugs taking orders from Galíndez in Eduardo Pavlovsky's *El señor Galíndez*, have a far more tenuous relationship to their authority figures. When the phone rings in *Passport*, Ott's stage directions indicate: "This is the most surprising sound in the world to the Soldier and Officer" (123). The Officer asks the voice on the other end, in vain, for information basic to a sense of national identity: "What's the President's name?" (125). Earlier, the Soldier has wondered: "we could be defending a border that doesn't even exist anymore" (119). Are the Soldier and the Officer defending a border, protecting a way of life, and ensuring domestic tranquility, or are they just off on a sadistic frolic of their own? Both on- and off-stage, as some national walls are torn down and others come up almost as quickly, the construction of borders is constantly under negotiation and may violently shift at any moment. Under these circumstances, the authority granted by the state's monopoly on the regulation of movement can easily facilitate a slide into violence for the sake of violence.

Nevertheless, the demand for documents that purportedly prove a human being's right to exist in a particular place on Earth at a particular time seems to grow ever more intense, as evidenced by the state of Arizona's 2010 passage of legislation that would require (had the law's constitutionality not been challenged in federal court) migrants to always carry documents proving their legal status. The passport, as in Ott's play, becomes a mechanism for legitimizing the very existence of the body. Conversely, without proper documents, the body becomes subject to all manner of assaults, subject to both legal and illegal persecution, and a stage on which others may create spectacles. Consider for instance the infamous Arizona Sheriff Arpaio and his use of what are essentially costumes to humiliate his detainees or the equally infamous orange jumpsuits used at Guantanamo to cast prisoners as "non-compliant." Equally ludicrous and also an instrument of attempted humiliation was the incessant demand from the so-called "birther movement" on the radical right to see President Obama's birth certificate, as if the repeated display of such a document could bestow legitimacy on a body that otherwise might not belong in a position of authority. Of course, the question and display are themselves an attempt to cast doubt on the legitimacy of Obama's authority to occupy the presidency. In *Passport*, Eugene's inability to produce proper documentation leads to the destruction of his sense of authority, of his sense of self.

Frank Möller describes a debate now raging in academic circles as the "looking/not looking dilemma" (1). When a body has been turned into a theater of suffering, what is the correct ethical response? One camp argues that we must look in order to serve as witnesses and so as not to, as art historian Stephen F. Eisenman makes the case in his book on the Abu Ghraib photographs, "ignore, or even to justify, however partially or provisionally, the facts of degradation and brutality manifest in the pictures" (9). The opposing camp argues that by looking we spectators become complicit in crime and cannot help but glean pleasure from the very pain we claim to condemn, turning ourselves into consumers of porn violence.[9] *Passport* chooses to look and to make us look, re-creating the images of Abu Ghraib through stage directions that mandate that the actor be leashed with a belt like a dog, hooded with a pointed black hood, attached to cables, and posed on a chair with his arms open. The Soldier snaps photos of his prisoner and of himself with his prisoner, reminding us of how the officers at Abu Ghraib took staged photos and filmed videos of themselves and their captives.

Having argued that part of the power and ethical integrity of Suárez's and LEGOM's works derives from their refusal to allow the spectator to indulge any prurient interest in brothels, am I now shifting my position to maintain that re-creations of the torture chamber, complete with powerless victims, are nevertheless non-exploitative? First, I would note that Ott's stage pictures are quite mild compared to many of the actual images of Abu Ghraib—the woman forced to lift her shirt to reveal her breasts, the men forced to masturbate (Eisenman 36-37). And second, I would argue that, depending on how the violence is framed, it is in fact possible to view pain inflicted on others without

---

[9] Theorists who argue along similar lines include Sontag, Boltanski, and Linfield. Theorists who stress the dangers of the gaze include Reinhardt and Hartman, who focuses not on photographs but on performative displays of African-American slave bodies.

taking pleasure in their humiliation or being overly self-congratulatory about the fact that we have escaped their fate ("It is not me, but it could be me"). This is perhaps the ethically ideal reaction for an aestheticized depiction of violence to elicit: a mid-range of identification in which the spectator is neither entirely seduced by the pleasure of intense-yet-temporary identification nor so completely aloof as to be indifferent or de-sensitized. In the mid-range, semi-identification continues after the gaze has been averted, after the narrative has concluded.

Several techniques with roots in Brechtian Epic Theatre, I would argue, help position *Passport* in this range: poetic language, a silent scream, and an open ending. Eugene could be us, as he meditates on his predicament:

Nothing like this ever happened to me before.

I thought things like this didn't really happen.

Maybe to other people. But not to me. (107)

In blank verse, not naturalistic speech, Eugene reminds spectators that we too could find ourselves ground up by the wheels of bureaucracy. After all, how many of us have now been forced to stand with legs spread and arms up before airport scanners, or patted down between the legs and under the breasts for the sake of national security? In the midst of Eugene's ordeal, the stage directions indicate, "The Officer takes off the hood. Eugene brings to mind Munch's *The Scream*" (109). The figure in the Edvard Munch painting in turn brings to mind the "silent scream" that Helene Weigel famously incorporated into her performance of Brecht's *Mother Courage*. Such a scream, unlike a realistic scream, invites us to reflect upon, as well as identify with, the pain of the screamer.

Over-identification is also discouraged by the fact that – unlike many victims in naturalistic or realistic plays, especially melodramas – Eugene is not depicted as morally superior by virtue of his suffering (Brooks 37). Contrary to the melodramatic tradition of displaying physical suffering as a sign of legible moral truth, Eugene's body seems to turn in on itself as a result of his ordeal. A monologue reveals that he has temporarily gone deaf and the sounds of his internal bodily functions have been magnified to the exclusion of all other sounds: the beating of his heart, the circulation of his blood through his veins, the batting of his eyelashes against his eyes. The monologue culminates in the image of a man fighting to maintain his sense of self: "And now? The sound of my thoughts. As they forge a path. As they rise up. As they try to be me" (118). In Teatro San Martín's 2003 Caracas production of *Passport*, the role of Eugene was played by a woman, María Brito, as "Eugenia," which may have prodded spectators to consider both whether women are more vulnerable than men to the vicissitudes of border patrol and how men are sometimes also feminized in situations of detention.

Finally, *Passport*'s circular ending, like the circular endings of *Matchmaker* and *Girls*, denies closure and catharsis to the spectator. Once Eugene discovers where he is – in his own country, it turns out – Eugene still doesn't recognize it. Do we recognize our country in the images of Abu Ghraib? Does the international passport system function merely to ascertain identity and maintain safe and orderly movement across national borders? Or, by threatening us with labels such as "illegal" and its consequences, does it also uphold those national borders and use fear to control the movement of our bodies-turned-spectacle? While in *Matchmaker* and *Girls* the embrace of the nation-state appears inadequate to protect its citizens, in *Passport* it proves positively venomous.

The dislocation of the protagonist from any particular country in Ott's work makes explicit what Suárez's and LEGOM's works implicitly suggest when read together: whether a body crosses vastly distant borders such as Poland and Argentina or dwells in the hazy borderlands between distant neighbors such as the United States and Mexico, the most important border it must constantly negotiate is the one between danger and safety.

Ana Elena Puga
The Ohio State University

Bibliography

Bixler, Jacqueline. "Games and Reality on the Latin American Stage." *Latin American Literary Review* 12.24 (1984): 22-35.

Boltanski, Luc. *Distant Suffering: Morality, Media and Politics.* Cambridge: Cambridge UP, 1997.

Brooks, Daphne A. *Bodies in Dissent: Spectacular Performances of Race and Freedom, 1850-1910.* Durham: Duke UP, 2006.

Castillo, Debra A. *Easy Women: Sex and Gender in Modern Mexican Fiction.* Minneapolis: Minnesota UP, 1998.

de la Mora, Sergio. *Cinemachismo: Masculinities and Sexuality in Mexican Film.* Austin: Texas UP, 2006.

Doezema, Jo. "Ouch!: Western Feminists' 'Wounded Attachment' to the 'Third World Prostitute.'" *Feminist Review* 67 (2001): 16-38.

Eisenman, Stephen F. *The Abu Ghraib Effect.* London: Reaktion Books, 2007.

Ferrari, Daniela. "Patricia Suárez: una trilogía polaca." *Cuadernos de Picadero* 5.15 (2008): 29-34.

Guy, Donna J. *Sex and Danger in Buenos Aires: Prostitution, Family, and Nation in Argentina*. Lincoln: Nebraska UP, 1991.

Hart, Lynda. *Making a Spectacle: Feminist Essays on Contemporary Women's Theatre*. Ann Arbor: Michigan UP, 1989.

Hartman, Sadiya V. *Scenes of Subjection*. New York and Oxford: Oxford UP, 1997.

Kartun, Mauricio. "Prologue." *Las polacas*. Patricia Suárez. Buenos Aires: Teatro Vivo, 2002. 3-5.

Larson, Catherine. "Playwrights of Passage: Women and Game-Playing on the Stage." *Latin American Literary Review* 19.38 (1991): 77-89.

Linfield, Susie. *The Cruel Radiance: Photography and Political Violence*. Chicago: U of Chicago P, 2010.

Magnarelli, Sharon. "Transitional Stages: Space and Illusion in *Las Polacas* by Patricia Suárez." *Trans/Acting: Latin American and Latino Performing Arts*. Eds. Jacqueline Bixler and Laurietz Seda. Lewisburg, PA: Bucknell UP, 2009. 37-54.

Möller, Frank. "The looking/not looking dilemma." *Review of International Studies* 35 (2009): 781-94.

Moreno Uribe, E.A. "El Prometeo de los 90: Gustavo Ott." *Sida, homosexualidad y otros teatros*. Caracas: Vadell Hermanos, 1993. 207-10.

Ong, Aihwa. "A Biocartography: Maids, Neoslavery, and NGOs." *Neoliberalism as Exception: Mutations in Citizenship and Sovereignty*. Durham: Duke UP, 2006. 195-217.

Phelan, Peggy. *Unmarked: The Politics of Performance*. London: Routledge, 1993.

Puga, Ana Elena. "Poor Enrique and Poor María, Or The Political Economy of Suffering in Two Migrant Melodramas." *Performance in the Borderlands*. Eds. Ramón Rivera-Servera and Harvey Young. New York: Palgrave Macmillan, 2011. 225-47.

Reinhardt, Mark. "Picturing Violence: Aesthetics and the Anxiety of Critique." *Beautiful Suffering: Photography and the Traffic in Pain*. Eds. Mark Reinhardt, Holly Edwards, and Erina Duganne. Williamstown/Chicago: Williams College Museum of Art/U of Chicago P, 2007. 13-36.

Rivera-Servera, Ramón H. and Harvey Young, eds. "Introduction." *Performance in the Borderlands*. New York: Palgrave Macmillan, 2011. 1-16.

Schneider, Elizabeth M. "Feminism and the False Dichotomy of Victimization and Agency." *New York Law School Law Review* 38 (1993): 387-99.

Schneider, Rebecca. *The Explicit Body in Performance*. London and New York: Routledge, 1997.

Solomon, Claire Thora. "Fictions of the 'Bad Life': The Discourse of Prostitution in Argentine Literature and Culture." Diss. Yale U, 2007. Web. 1 April 2011.

Sontag, Susan. *Regarding the Pain of Others.* New York: Farrar, Straus and Giroux, 2002.

Torpey, John. *The Invention of the Passport: Surveillance, Citizenship and the State.* Cambridge: Cambridge UP, 2000.

United States. Dept. of State. *Trafficking in Persons Report 2010.* Washington, DC: US Dept. of State, 2010.

Vincent, Isabel. *Bodies and Souls: The Tragic Plight of Three Jewish Women Forced into Prostitution in the Americas.* New York: Harper Collins, 2005.

MATCHMAKER

PATRICIA SUÁREZ

translated by
ANA ELENA PUGA

Left to right: Rocío Speranza, Paula García, and Estefanía Arzú, in *Matchmaker*, CEARTE Youth Theater production in 2007, Trenque Lauquen, Argentina. Photo courtesy of Luis Cabrera, Artistic Director of CEARTE.

Characters

The matchmaker. GOLDE. 50 years old.

The groom. SCHLOMO. A wealthy man, elegant, somewhat bald. About 35/40 years old.

EDIT/ADA. Very beautiful, glowing, about 25 years old. She is an idiot. She is lost all the time, managing with great difficulty to articulate a few words. Then, as ADA, she is a normal girl, almost sullen.

EMMA. 17 years old. Attractive without being beautiful. Very young. A smooth talker.

Matchmaker [*Casamentera*] was first produced at the Patio de Actores in Buenos Aires on June 1, 2002 with the following cast and production team.

GOLDE	Alejandra Molinari
SCHLOMO	Jorge Sánchez Mon
EDIT/ADA	Georgina Rey
EMMA	Flavia Sinsky
DIRECTOR	Elvira Onetto
ASSISTANT DIRECTOR	Martín Flores Cárdenas
SCENIC DESIGN/LIGHTING	Gabriel Caputo
COSTUMES	Emilio Abrodos
MUSIC	Patricia Martínez
SOUND OPERATOR	Pablo Flores Cárdenas

This translation is based on the Spanish-language version published as: Suárez, Patricia. *Las polacas: Historias tártaras, Casamentera, La Varsovia.* Buenos Aires: Teatro Vivo, 2002. Some colloquial expressions and proverbs were changed with the permission of the author.

1920. A village in Poland.

The action always occurs in the living room of the matchmaker's house. A window with lace curtains allows for a view of the street and the snow. There are three or four silk screens, imitation Japanese, which allow the various characters to move behind them and speak privately. It seems that behind one of the screens is a bed with a sick boy, Moishe. Outside it is cold, maybe ten degrees below freezing or more.

1

Schlomo sits on a little armchair. An air of propriety, a little uncomfortable. Golde, very dressed up, serves tea from the samovar. She always speaks in a very low voice.

GOLDE: Pretty. Above all, pretty. *(Schlomo nods.)* Blonde. *(Schlomo nods.)* With long hair, very long, so that it covers her back. Is that how you want her?

SCHLOMO: Yes.

GOLDE: And young, of an age to marry.

SCHLOMO: Yes.

GOLDE: Mr. Trauman wrote to me saying that you would settle the final details with me...

SCHLOMO: What details?

GOLDE: Lower your voice, please. My little Moishe is there. *(She points behind a screen.)* He's sick. Trifles, small expenses... you can't expect to conquer a girl with gifts of sighs and breezes.

SCHLOMO: What is wrong with your son?

GOLDE: *(Very sad.)* His lungs. They don't work right.

SCHLOMO: Oh.

GOLDE: The doctors ask a fortune of me... and I... I don't have a single kopeck. If it weren't for Mr. Trauman's help, really...

SCHLOMO: What did the doctors tell you?

GOLDE: That he will recover. But his father, my husband, died of the same thing. One day he couldn't breathe.

SCHLOMO: Oh. I have a few rubles here, for you if you need them, I would like to help you.

(Schlomo gives her money.)

GOLDE: Thank you. I wouldn't ask if I had a few rubles available in my purse for this matter of the girl. The bride, as you say.

SCHLOMO: I thought everything had been foreseen.

GOLDE: Oh, oh. You are a child at heart. Love can never be foreseen. It's just a few more rubles. The father is reluctant. He is mistrustful.

SCHLOMO: I have a proxy.[1] In Argentina we will be married by a rabbi.

GOLDE: More tea?

SCHLOMO: No, thank you.

(Golde serves herself tea.)

GOLDE: Perhaps Mr. Trauman sent me some... how is it called there? Green gold?

SCHLOMO: Yes. Green gold, in Brazil; not in Argentina. I left it at my cousin Ester's house. He also sent you chocolate. Tomorrow I can bring it to you.

GOLDE: And how is he?

SCHLOMO: Mr. Trauman? His businesses are going well. To see him, one must make an appointment three days in advance and sometimes even then he will not see you: that's how busy he is.

GOLDE: May God keep him wealthy. And his health? A relative of mine wrote me that he suffered from a secret illness, no...?

SCHLOMO: He was cured by a patent medicine.

GOLDE: Oh. What was the patent medicine called?

SCHLOMO: Lambert, it cures in three days.

---

[1] In other words, he has a document that permits him to marry a young woman despite the absence of her father. To avoid confusion, in production the word "license" or "release" might be substituted for "proxy."

GOLDE: Oh, that's good. I always say: God helps the clever. I've some fresh-baked little cakes: surely you would like one.

SCHLOMO: No, Mrs. Golde. Thank you, I don't have an appetite.

GOLDE: Do you think you can conquer a girl when you are thin as a reed? It will just be a moment. *(Golde goes out. She returns after a short while with a tray full of little cakes, chewing on one. She goes behind the screen and commands sweetly.)* Just one, Moishe. They're made the way you like them. *(During the rest of the scene she continually eats pastries and speaks with her mouth full.)* And how is your cousin Ester? I put cinnamon on them, try them.

SCHLOMO: Very well.

GOLDE: *(To the screen.)* Do you like them, Moishe? *(To Schlomo, very low.)* He doesn't answer; he's eating. I left him three cakes; it's a trial to feed him. Is she your mother's cousin or your mother's aunt? I don't remember the relationship very well.

SCHLOMO: She's my father's second cousin. A cousin by marriage, as they say. The one who lived in Austria.

GOLDE: She's very kind to receive you. *(Schlomo agrees. As she savors a cake.)* We aren't getting very good cinnamon. They smuggle it in from Hungary... And you think she is discreet this, your cousin Ester?

SCHLOMO: Yes.

GOLDE: Beware of her.

SCHLOMO: I don't think...

GOLDE: She's an old fox. Who do you think wrote an anonymous note to Rabbi Itzak disclosing that the son of the shoemaker was not really the son of the shoemaker, but rather an adventure on the part of the shoemaker's wife?

SCHLOMO: My cousin?

(Golde nods.)

GOLDE: Do not listen to a word from your cousin Ester! *(Long pause. Schlomo starts to eat cakes.)* They're tasty, right?

(Schlomo nods.)

SCHLOMO: What is she like?

GOLDE: Friede?

SCHLOMO: Her name is Friede?

GOLDE: Since she was born.

SCHLOMO: It's not a very pretty name. *(Golde shrugs.)* And how is Friede?

GOLDE: She suffered lasting damage from that terrible beating the shoemaker gave her. She lost two fingers...

SCHLOMO: *(In horror.)* Friede?

GOLDE: And what would you have done, Mr. Schlomo, if your wife brought you a child that wasn't yours?

SCHLOMO: I was asking about the girl you were telling me about...

(Schlomo, exasperated, serves himself tea and sips. Golde smiles coquettishly.)

GOLDE: I think it needs a few more leaves. Don't you think? *(Schlomo doesn't answer.)* This year was very rough, not even a single wheat stalk grew... Do you have children?

SCHLOMO: No ma'am. I'm here to get married.

GOLDE: I know, don't lose your temper. And speak softly, please. Moishe had a fever this morning. But you could still have children. Mr. Trauman has sent me such men – you can't even imagine!

SCHLOMO: *(Tired.)* Ma'am, I...

GOLDE: Her name is Edit.

SCHLOMO: Edit.

GOLDE: Edit Volf.

SCHLOMO: *(Very slowly.)* I like it. Did you tell her to come?

GOLDE: She's very frightened of her father.

SCHLOMO: Oh.

GOLDE: You'll see, she's a very shy girl. But you can see her. She takes her family's two cows out to pasture. Yes. Up on the hillside. Early in the morning.

Schlomo: May I speak to her?

Golde: She has a big sweet-tooth. Take her some sweets.

Schlomo: Certainly. *(He begins to get up.)* I shall take my leave...

Golde: You know something? I need five rubles. For those expenses on trifles that I mentioned to you... for a silk ribbon for her hair, she would like to have that...

Schlomo: *(Rummaging through his wallet, unperturbed.)* Five rubles?

Golde: *(Extending her hand.)* Seven would be better.

Schlomo: A hair ribbon costs seven rubles?

Golde: Darling, I've told you already how life in our village is impossible. *(Schlomo gives her the bills. She accompanies him and closes the door. Then she sits at the table and counts the money. Once, twice, three times, relentlessly, wetting the tips of her fingers.)* One, two, how can we make do? Three, four... we need so much more... Oh, you lost your place, Golde, child, you're always such a fool.

2

The same characters.

It is dawn; Golde comes out in a robe with her hair covered by a nightcap. Schlomo enters, furious. The tone of the entire scene is one of tension and fury.

Golde: Mr. Schlomo, what is it? It's snowing!

Schlomo: I don't like her.

Golde: What? Come in, come in, speak softly. The baby is asleep.

Schlomo: I saw her.

Golde: Who?

Schlomo: Edit Volf, I went to the hillside, as you told me, and I saw her. I don't like her.

Golde: She played hard to get.

Schlomo: No.

GOLDE: Ah, no?

SCHLOMO: No.

GOLDE: And so why don't you like her?

SCHLOMO: She's an imbecile.

GOLDE: Isn't it a bit hasty to say...?

SCHLOMO: She drools. *(Pause.)* The drool ran down her jaw.

GOLDE: Oh. Still, maybe...

SCHLOMO: She sucked her finger. Her thumb. All the time.

GOLDE: Did you speak to her?

SCHLOMO: Yes.

GOLDE: What did she say?

SCHLOMO: Nothing. She only said her name. Edit.

GOLDE: Edit is a marvelous name. You said so yourself.

SCHLOMO: She is an idiot. You did not inform me. How am I going to marry an idiot-woman?

GOLDE: She is very sweet.

SCHLOMO: She is an idiot! An idiot will not do!

GOLDE: Do not shout, please, I beg of you. My son is very sick. And what do you care whether she is an idiot or a wise woman?

SCHLOMO: No one wants anything to do with an idiot.

GOLDE: That's not right.

SCHLOMO: An idiot inspires pity.

GOLDE: Don't you believe it. In Krialovitz, where my father was from, there was a girl who only knew how to count to five and...

SCHLOMO: Mr. Trauman is not going to like it if I bring an idiot. *(Long pause.)* He pays a fortune for her and it turns out that...

GOLDE: *(Dejected.)* She has nine sisters. Pick one of the sisters.

SCHLOMO: The sisters! And are they normal, by any chance, these sisters? *(He paces anxiously.)* I don't know.

GOLDE: She will come here to meet with you.

SCHLOMO: The idiot?

GOLDE: She won't come alone. She can't come alone to meet with a man.

SCHLOMO: I realize that. It's a miracle that she takes the animals out to pasture and doesn't lose them...

GOLDE: I was going to bring Anna, one of her sisters, already married. Anna is a flower, also. And childbirth has not ruined her figure! Perhaps you would like to meet her.

SCHLOMO: Who?

GOLDE: Anna.

SCHLOMO: The married one? For what?

GOLDE: I don't know. For a good time.

SCHLOMO: What are you talking about? I don't want to indulge in a good time, madam. I have come to marry.

GOLDE: She's just like Edit. She's a beauty. Identical, what they call two drops of water. You are not going to deny to me that Edit is very beautiful? The village flower.

SCHLOMO: She is an idiot.

GOLDE: Yes, yes, you told me so already. You don't want to meet Anna then?

SCHLOMO: No.

GOLDE: Wait for me for a moment. I'm going to make sure that the boy is asleep. *(She goes behind the screen.)* Like an angel. He's not getting better. He has me so worried. Pan[2] Mendel needs the dowry that you will pay for his daughter. He has ten mouths to feed.

SCHLOMO: Madam, I am not a mutual aid society.

---

2   "Pan" is an honorific title in Yiddish equivalent to the English "Mr."

GOLDE: Yes, yes. *(Pause.)* Perhaps you would be interested in Alma. Oh, if you haven't seen Alma you don't know what a beautiful girl is! She is a few years younger than Edit, but they are like Leah and Rachel.

SCHLOMO: *(Interested.)* Which of the two is Rachel?

GOLDE: Alma, my dear.

SCHLOMO: Leah was cross-eyed and had a huge body.

GOLDE: Let's not repeat things that...

SCHLOMO: Rachel was dark-skinned.

GOLDE: Same as Alma, who has long black hair...

SCHLOMO: *(Interrupting.)* In Argentina they favor blondes.

GOLDE: *(Without listening to him.)*... She is small in size, but when she grows up...

SCHLOMO: How old is she?

GOLDE: Fourteen.

SCHLOMO: Fourteen!!

GOLDE: Lower your voice, please.

SCHLOMO: Fourteen is a very young age for a woman. I don't...

GOLDE: But she doesn't look it. To see her, one thinks right away she's an older girl. Besides, you can wait a couple of years until she turns...

SCHLOMO: A couple of years? Where? Here?

GOLDE: Then marry Alma now.

SCHLOMO: What do you think? You think I'm a monster?

GOLDE: *(Softly.)* Oh, oh, oh. It seems as if no one will do for you!!

(Long pause. Schlomo looks out of a window.)

SCHLOMO: *(Nervous.)* It snows, and snows, and snows. Do you have anything to drink?

GOLDE: I'll go get vodka.

(Golde exits. She returns with a bottle and two little glasses. She tries to be gay. Schlomo drinks two glasses, one after another. Gradually they will both get drunk.)[3]

SCHLOMO: *(Angry.)* Did you ever arrange anyone's marriage?

GOLDE: Me? If I start to tell you now we wouldn't even finish by dawn tomorrow.

SCHLOMO: You know I've got to take a woman to Argentina.

GOLDE: Did you live in the Ukraine, Mr. Schlomo?

SCHLOMO: Yes, why?

GOLDE: Say it in Ukrainian then. I don't remember how you say "to take" in Ukrainian... to go is... let me see... no, I don't remember. A shame. I'm sure it rhymed.

SCHLOMO: I left the village at the age of thirteen.

GOLDE: But what language did they speak in your village?

SCHLOMO: When am I gonna see 'em?

GOLDE: Who?

SCHLOMO: The idiot Edit Volf and her sister.

GOLDE: Tomorrow. *(She drinks.)* So you're interested after all.

SCHLOMO: No.

GOLDE: She's very beautiful. You can't deny it. *(She gargles with vodka.)* When my breath smelled of vodka my Moishe's father didn't want to kiss me. Evil beast!

---

[3]   Up to this point in the scene, I have used contractions sparingly to indicate both the formality of the situation and the fact that the play takes place almost a hundred years ago, when use of contractions in proper English was less common. As the characters drink, their speech becomes less formal. In a later scene (Scene Four), I follow a similar logic, with the turning point being the moment Schlomo threatens Golde with the scissors. My sense is that after that moment, because most of the pretense between them has been dropped, their use of contractions increases. In production, actors and directors may want to experiment with adding or deleting contractions in order to create effects such as fluidity of speech, intensity of emotion, emphasis on negative intention (for instance, "will not" or "cannot") as well as degree of intimacy or distance (AEP).

SCHLOMO: Find me a good girl, Golde. A pretty one, of course. Blonde, if possible. And intelligent... Let her be merry. A merry woman with a warm heart and a womb...

GOLDE: A merry woman, Mr. Schlomo... A flower. A rose...

(Blackout.)

makes us think that he really is looking for someone

citizen vs worker in Argentina

vs populate Argentina

3

Schlomo, Golde, Edit, and Emma. The small sitting room.

Schlomo and the girls, Edit and her sister Emma, talk behind a screen.

EMMA: ... And then father told her to get down, but she was scared so she kept climbing higher and higher, until she was almost at the top. So it was mother... my mother doesn't have much patience for these things. So she went with a stick, and she poked it around in the leaves until she managed to tangle up Edit's skirt and make her fall. Then she hit her head. *(To Edit.)* Wasn't that how it was, Edit? *(Pause.)* She was in bed for I don't know how many months... *(To Edit.)* Was it four months or actually closer to a year, Edit? *(Pause.)* She doesn't know. I think it was four. *(To Edit.)* What is it? Later. *(To Schlomo.)* Father was very sad. Edit is so beautiful! And a pretty face is half the dowry, father says.

SCHLOMO: You're very pretty too. You are a red rose.

EMMA: Thank you. *(To Edit.)* Not right now. No.

EDIT: *(Shouts.)* Bathroom!

EMMA: Later! *(To Schlomo.)* Do you know how Mrs. Golde's boy is doing?

SCHLOMO: Badly, I believe.

how edit and emma relate to eachother vs have a connection (giggling)

EMMA: His lungs are not well.

SCHLOMO: So I heard.

vs at same time fighting emma saying that she hates her.

EMMA: From the boy???

vs competition.

SCHLOMO: Mrs. Golde.

EMMA: The doctors can't find a cure. She is very beloved in our town.

SCHLOMO: Oh, really?

emma takes command so he is more drawn to him.

EMMA: The girls like her a lot. She has already married several who went to Argentina. It must be a beautiful country. I'm sure Edit would have been very happy in Argentina. *(To Edit.)* Isn't that right, Edit? *(To Schlomo.)* She doesn't know what Argentina means. *(To Edit.)* It's a country, like Russia or like Poland. *(To Schlomo.)* Is Argentina pretty?

SCHLOMO: Yes.

EMMA: What do they eat?

SCHLOMO: Beef.

EMMA: Beef? I was told that the main dish was potato stew. And beans.

SCHLOMO: It's not true. Beef and pork.

EMMA: But you don't eat pork, right?

SCHLOMO: Yes.

EMMA: Yes?

SCHLOMO: No. No, I don't like pork.

EMMA: We don't eat pork, either; Father would never allow it. And what do you do in Argentina? *(Pause.)* What sort of work do you do?

SCHLOMO: I'm in the skin trade.

EMMA: The skin trade, how wonderful! Did you hear, Edit? He's in the skin trade! Like the husbands of Berta and Martita! Do you know them? Berta and Martita went to Argentina, one of them a year ago and the other the year before. Their husbands were skin traders too! You can tell that it's cold in Argentina with such a large market for skin. *(To Edit.)* What furs was it they sold? *(To Schlomo.)* She doesn't know. She never remembers anything.

(A mild fight develops, in which Edit pulls Emma's hair and Emma responds with hair pulling and pinching.)

EMMA: Stupid!

SCHLOMO: Don't yell, remember the boy...

EMMA: *(Composing herself.)* Yes, yes. It's just that she's an idiot. I can't stand her. Here it's very expensive to have a fur coat made. In Russia, they use bear, but we can't buy it. Only beaver. Mother says if we had fur coats the winter wouldn't make us suffer so. We had two little brothers before, who would help Papa a little: Leopold and Micael. They were darling boys. *(To Edit.)* Isn't that so, Edit? *(Edit nods.)* But they couldn't withstand the winter and the bad food... like Mrs. Golde's son. *(Pause.)* The winter kills too many people here. *(Edit doubles over and whimpers like a two-year-old child.)* Father was leaving for town with my two little brothers, to the inn. They were both very little at that time. He would act like a drunk: he'd take bets on who would get drunk first, Leopold or Pan Meyer's turkey. They would give Leopold vodka with milk and give the turkey grain alcohol and breadcrumbs. The town folk would laugh at these things. Leopold would always get drunk, then he would start banging his head against the walls. Afterwards they would kill the turkey with a little knife. And they would eat it. *(Pause.)* That's why father didn't love Leopold and he did love Micael, because Micael would never get drunk and he'd help him win his bets. Later they died, one after the other, Leopold when he was nine and Micael when he was ten. Mother almost died of sadness and so did I. *(Long pause.)* Don't start! *(To Schlomo.)* I hate her. *(To Edit.)* Shut up. *(To Schlomo.)* She remembers our little brothers. The cold was to blame, I swear to you. This year it killed seven people in our town, and this is a small town... And it never stops snowing! It's been snowing for three days straight, and my sisters and I have holes in our boots...

SCHLOMO: *(Fawning.)* If you would allow me to I could help you to mend the boots...

EMMA: *(Without paying much attention.)* Is it very cold in Argentina?

SCHLOMO: No. Here. *(He takes money out of his billfold and holds it out toward Emma, who takes it timidly and tucks it away in her bosom; then, with an effort, he tries to make conversation.)* I live in Rosario. By the side of a river. I have a... little house. Pretty. Three times a week I go to the movie palace. I watch the news reel and a film... Have you ever been to a movie palace?

EMMA: No.

SCHLOMO: You will love it. It's like dreaming, you know?

EMMA: They told me it was nice.

SCHLOMO: Who told you?

EMMA: Martita. She wrote me and she told me. But she says she doesn't have much time to go.

SCHLOMO: Where does your friend Martita live?

EMMA: In Argentina.

SCHLOMO: Yes. You'd already told me that. I was asking what city she lives in.

EMMA: Sorry. This idiot is contagious. Melosa, I think it's called.

SCHLOMO: Melosa?

EMMA: It's near the mountains. Higher than the Carpathians, she says.

SCHLOMO: Mendoza.

EMMA: I don't know. She wrote Melosa.

SCHLOMO: She might have written it incorrectly.

EMMA: *(Bored.)* She's very stupid. I think she's sick in the head. Do people in Argentina fall ill often?

SCHLOMO: *(Thinking.)* No.

EMMA: No?

SCHLOMO: No. Because of the climate. It never snows there. And the people eat fairly well. It's a rich country.

EMMA: Rich in what way?

SCHLOMO: The streets are strewn with gold. The thing is you have to know how to pick it up without getting run over.

EMMA: And you? Are you sickly?

SCHLOMO: No. And did you ever get sick?

EMMA: In eighteen years I've never once had a fever.

SCHLOMO: How old are you, Emma?

EMMA: Me?

SCHLOMO: Yes.

EMMA: Eighteen.

SCHLOMO: You seem younger.

EMMA: Because of the milk skin. When I can and father isn't watching, I rub milk skin on my face. They say that's good for it.

SCHLOMO: I am certain you would like Argentina.

EMMA: Me too.

SCHLOMO: Would you like to come?

EMMA: I don't know.

EDIT: Bathroom!!

EMMA: I told you no. Be still! *(To Schlomo.)* It's terrible. When she gets like this, mother ties her to the birch.

SCHLOMO: *(Shocked.)* She ties her to a tree?

EMMA: Not in winter, no. So she doesn't get sick. Because otherwise later you spend double the money calling the doctor to fix the harm done by the cold. Mother doesn't like for us single girls to go to the doctor. She didn't even send Leopold or Micael to the doctor when they got sick. It's too expensive, you understand? *(Pause.)* But in summer she does tie her. Mother says the sun calms her. She looks at the sun and she calms down. Enough! *(To Schlomo.)* But this one is so furious! She has such strength! Once when she was tied up she even yanked the birch out by the roots! Father says we should send her to the forests, so she can help the woodsmen... *(To Edit, who pulls Emma's hair and pinches her furiously.)* Enough! Enough!

(Emma stands up and hits her. Edit defends herself. They fight. Schlomo tries to separate them.)

SCHLOMO: Young ladies! Young ladies, please! Emma, Emma! Leave her!

(They sit.)

EMMA: I'm sorry. But she's an imbecile. You would have gone crazy if you had taken her to Argentina. You're right to leave her here; she's not for you.

SCHLOMO: No. I saw your sister in a picture... that Mrs. Golde sent to my uncle Noé...

EMMA: Mr. Trauman?

SCHLOMO: Yes. And I want to marry, you know? To start a family.

(Emma nods.)

EMMA: Edit looks very good in photographs.

SCHLOMO: But I hadn't seen you. Otherwise I would have picked you. *(Long pause.)* You wouldn't... I mean, wouldn't you agree... wouldn't you agree to come to... to marry me... in Argentina?

EMMA: *(Disturbed.)* I don't know.

SCHLOMO: Why not? In Argentina I will feed you sweets. You will live as happy as a bird. *(Emma leans over and speaks some inaudible words into her sister's ear. Then they laugh roguishly.)* You will never have a single worry with me, Emma.

EMMA: Like a bird. *(To Edit.)* You're jealous! *(Laughs. To Schlomo.)* You should speak to my father.

SCHLOMO: *(Content.)* You accept?

(Emma nods.)

EMMA: But my father... my father... you know? He had the idea that you would leave with Edit and... and now...

SCHLOMO: That's not going to be a problem, Emma. *(Schlomo, happy, gets up from his seat, goes toward Emma, lifts her up by the elbows.)* Permit me to kiss you.

(Schlomo moves closer to kiss her. She reacts timidly. At that moment Emma starts to lift her feet. There is a puddle of urine under her feet. It is Edit. She has urinated, wetting the sofa, the floor, herself.)

EMMA: *(To Edit.)* What did you do?! Couldn't you hold on? *(Shakes her sister.)* Disgusting! Disgusting! What a stench! You embarrass me.

(She starts to hit her sister; Edit cries.)

(Blackout.)

4

The small living room in shadows. Schlomo and Golde.

SCHLOMO: Make arrangements with the father.

GOLDE: Pan Mendel is distrustful. The money you're offering isn't enough for him. *(To the little boy.)* Moishe, how are you?

SCHLOMO: Mr. Trauman paid three thousand pesos for a woman.

GOLDE: He paid three thousand pesos for Edit Volf not for Emma, Mr. Schlomo. *(To her little son.)* Moishe!

SCHLOMO: Edit is much more beautiful, you know it.

GOLDE: Me? Yes, of course I know it.

SCHLOMO: Edit is very beautiful.

GOLDE: I was the one who offered her to you, don't forget. Moishe! For the love of God! What are you doing?

SCHLOMO: Emma has a crooked nose.

GOLDE: Crooked? I hadn't noticed.

SCHLOMO: And she is bow-legged. She lifted her skirt...

GOLDE: *(Interrupting.)* She lifted her skirt?

SCHLOMO: To show me a scar on her knee... and... she has very skinny legs!

GOLDE: What do you want? In this village we hardly eat.

SCHLOMO: She has no meat on her legs! And her forehead! So high! From a distance she looks like a bald woman.

GOLDE: Then look at her up close.

SCHLOMO: And her freckles? You know that freckles in a woman are not attractive.

GOLDE: Make her wash herself with rosewater... or with lemon, every morning.

SCHLOMO: What? What does rosewater have to do with anything? I am talking about beauty, about loveliness. How could Emma be worth more than her sister, Mrs. Golde?

GOLDE: Take Edit Volf.

SCHLOMO: I liked Emma.

GOLDE: Emma is worth more. Wait for me a moment, my Moishe isn't talking. Let me see what's going on. *(Exits. Goes behind the screen where Moishe supposedly is.)* What? Which little horsey, my son? Which dapple-gray? At the fair! Of course, my love, of course. This very Sunday, of course. *(She returns downhearted.)* He's delirious. *(Golde cries.)* Do you think he'll die?

SCHLOMO: *(Concerned.)* No...

GOLDE: *(To the heavens.)* Why? Why, my God?

(Long silence.)

SCHLOMO: Ma'am... I... I want Emma.

GOLDE: *(Recovered.)* Emma helps the family churning the butter. What do you want, Mr. Schlomo? The whole town is like this, dying of hunger. Who will make the butter in Pan Mendel's house, if you take the girl?

SCHLOMO: Some boy, maybe...

GOLDE: No, no. There are no boys in October. They've all found work already. They would have to bring one from Gërtha. That's very expensive. You're going to have to pay more for Emma: she'll make you a tidy profit in the end, you'll see. Besides, you've seen: she knows how to make entertaining conversation. That means many more rubles for your business. She will entertain the clients...

SCHLOMO: I don't want her to entertain the clients.

GOLDE: *(Surprised.)* No?

SCHLOMO: I want her for myself.

GOLDE: Really? For you?

SCHLOMO: I want to marry her.

GOLDE: You?

SCHLOMO: Yes.

GOLDE: How strange. You've fallen in love?

SCHLOMO: Yes.

GOLDE: Just like that, all of a sudden? How did this happen? Had you decided to fall in love before you left Buenos Aires?

SCHLOMO: As soon as it stops snowing, I'll leave with Emma on the first train.

GOLDE: Here it will snow without stopping for at least a month, maybe two. October is always like that. Don't be in a hurry.

SCHLOMO: I'll hire a coach.

GOLDE: Just a minute. *(Exits, goes behind the screen. Returns downhearted.)* You should have come here sooner, in July or August. Now it won't stop snowing. No driver will want to cross the snow with you on board. Many have frozen to death because they played the hero in the heart of October. Why did you come so late, Mr. Schlomo? What kept you in Warsaw? The cards or the dice?

SCHLOMO: My mother. My mother was dying in Warsaw. She died when I arrived. She had been waiting for me. Anxiously.

GOLDE: Your mother?

SCHLOMO: If it weren't for her, Mr. Trauman would have sent someone else instead of me. Zelig Rubenstein. But I wanted to see my mother before she died.

GOLDE: Your mother was Mr. Trauman's sister?

SCHLOMO: Yes.

GOLDE: You had told me that he wasn't your uncle.

SCHLOMO: To my mother he is dead. *(Pause.)* To my mother all those who go to Argentina are dead.

(Golde gets up, paces.)

GOLDE: Look, I don't know nor do I care what is going through your head, Mr. Schlomo. Nor whether you want Emma for the brothel or as the mother of your children. If you were in such a hurry, you should have come to the town sooner. Mr. Trauman sends me money during the year so that I can arrange things with the girl and the father. He wrote that you would come to our town by the month of August. I have an agreement with Mr. Trauman. I arranged things with Edit Volf, the pearl of the young women; you didn't like her. To scorn a girl because she is not as bright as you would like is a lack of imagination, sir. Now you want the sister. Emma Volf churns the butter for her family; they live from the butter and cheese they sell at market. Without Emma, they will have to hire a helper, do you understand? Where are they going to find a boy in the middle of October? The sister is worth more, Mr. Schlomo.

SCHLOMO: Mr. Trauman is not going to pay a single penny more for her.

GOLDE: *(Annoyed.)* A penny?

SCHLOMO: A kopeck.

GOLDE: Ah. Emma Volf is worth more than her sister. If Mr. Trauman does not pay, you will pay. If not, she will not leave the village.

SCHLOMO: She wants to go.

GOLDE: They all want to go. Or do you think they are enjoying their hunger here? But you've already seen how this business of marriage-by-proxy smells so fishy to the police...

SCHLOMO: I plan to marry her, here or in... in the same coach that takes us to Warsaw; you shall come and we shall take your son to be examined by the best doctor in the city. To cure him. The expenses are no object.

GOLDE: No.

(Long pause.)

SCHLOMO: How much more for Emma?

GOLDE: Double.

SCHLOMO: You're crazy!

GOLDE: Double. And about 150 rubles for Moishe's doctor.

(Pause. Schlomo walks around the room, takes a scissors from a sewing basket, threatens Golde from a distance.)

SCHLOMO: And if I kill you?

GOLDE: Me? The police have been warned. They especially hate people like you...

(Schlomo puts down the scissors.)

SCHLOMO: One thousand five hundred more.

GOLDE: Two thousand five hundred.

SCHLOMO: One thousand eight hundred.

GOLDE: Two thousand. And the expenses for the boy.

SCHLOMO: Two thousand.

GOLDE: All right. *(She paces.)* When will you give it to me?

SCHLOMO: It'll take a week to arrive from London.

GOLDE: A week. That's fine... Now, tell me, did you really fall in love with Emma? *(Schlomo doesn't answer.)* Are you embarrassed to confide in me? Do you think Emma Volf will fall in love with you? *(Pause.)* Fine. Keep it to yourself. *(Long pause.)* Tell me, Mr. Schlomo, what do you think will happen when she realizes that you had at first selected her for a brothel?

SCHLOMO: *(Uncomfortable.)* She won't know.

GOLDE: And how will you hide your activities from her?

SCHLOMO: I told her that I'm a furrier.

GOLDE: You all say the same thing. It must seem very elegant to you to refer to a woman as a "skin." Who was it that lacked originality? Mr. Trauman or Mr. Migdal?

SCHLOMO: I'll buy furs when I get to Warsaw. Ermines. Minks. She'll trust me.

GOLDE: Oh, oh.

SCHLOMO: I don't live in the zone with the brothels: I live further out, on the outskirts. I have a little house, painted with lime, with a little garden... An old woman lives with me, a Spanish woman, she cooks for me, cleans the house, waters the plants... There's a vegetable garden in the back, with pumpkin, onion, and cabbage... there's a chicken house that isn't being used, when Emma comes we can have hens and chickens...

GOLDE: A landowner!

SCHLOMO: Excuse me?

GOLDE: Nothing, nothing. See how it snows?

SCHLOMO: *(Disconcerted.)* Yes... always the same.

GOLDE: No, no. Go and look. *(Schlomo approaches a window, contemplates the snow.)* See how the snow falls.

SCHLOMO: I don't see anything in particular about how the snow falls.

GOLDE: Exactly. It always falls. That's what I want to say to you. *(Pause.)* How long do you think you can hide it from Emma Volf? Months, a year?

SCHLOMO: I don't care.

GOLDE: And now what will you do in Argentina with Mr. Trauman? Will you say to him, "You see, Uncle Noé, I was going to look for a skin for you but instead I brought myself back a wife"? Do you think he'll take it well?

SCHLOMO: I'll give him back the money.

GOLDE: So Mr. Schlomo is a gentleman of means!

SCHLOMO: Shut up.

GOLDE: How many times have you already made this trip? Five? Six times? You are a gentleman of a certain age; you must have been doing this for the last twenty-five years. How many girls have you taken to Argentina? Twelve? Ten?

SCHLOMO: *(Somber.)* Five.

GOLDE: Five. Five wives? And where are they?

SCHLOMO: I don't know.

GOLDE: Did they retire from the trade?

SCHLOMO: Bronia Kaufman, yes. She was very old.

GOLDE: And the others?

SCHLOMO: The others?

GOLDE: Yes.

SCHLOMO: I don't know, madam. I just take them, that's all.

GOLDE: I won't reveal anything to our Emma if you tell me where Rut Rosenbaum is. You took her, right? She was from the Ukraine, like you. From Kámenets-Podolsk.

SCHLOMO: *(Trying to remember.)* Rut...?

GOLDE: In her village, her mother asks after her.

SCHLOMO: *(Recollecting.)* Rut's mother...?

GOLDE: She is my sister. Her mother is my sister. You went to look for a "skin," but fancied my sister's daughter. Rut Rosenbaum. You told my sister that you had fallen in love with her, with little Rut. My sister handed over her daughter in full confidence, at the same price of the "skin" you had gone to look for. My sister was so stupid. Even today she doesn't forgive herself. She torments herself. She's wasted away with guilt. *(Pause.)* Her daughter had very long blonde hair; when she undid her braids, her hair went down to the back of her knees. When she was a girl, she loved nothing more than to climb trees... Her eyes were gray, I think... gray. She was merry. She sang. She knew songs in Yiddish and some parts of Yiddish plays. She had learned them from a rabbi who visited the Ukraine on his way back from England. That's what they said. That the rabbi taught them to her out of love. He was a very old and very jolly man. Songs in Yiddish. Do you know any?

(Long pause.)

SCHLOMO: *(Recalls.)* Rut Rosenbaum. She is dead. She poisoned herself. *(Long pause, then when he sees Golde's dismay.)* No, no. Long after arriving in Argentina. She was with Zwi... Zusman. She worked for him. In Junín. Later he left her... I think it was then that she...

GOLDE: He mistreated her.

(Golde exits. She goes to see her son. She returns, dries her tears with a handkerchief. She collapses into an armchair and cries.)
(Blackout.)

The little living room. Golde, Emma, and Edit Volf (as Ada). Ada looks different: at first she gives the impression of being calmer; gradually the nature of Edit's identity is revealed to the spectator.

GOLDE: So everything is all ready?

EMMA: Yes.

GOLDE: The passports, the suitcases?

EMMA: I have so little in the suitcase, Mrs. Golde...!

GOLDE: You will have more.

EMMA: We're going by train to Paris and will stay there for three days. To sightsee and stretch our legs. Schlomo says that if everything is calm we'll board the ship in Marseilles.

GOLDE: What does it mean that a city like Marseilles is calm?

EMMA: Without storm clouds, he told me.

GOLDE and EDIT: Oh.

EMMA: Then we're going to England. We'll leave from Liverpool.

GOLDE and EDIT: *(Applauding.)* Liverpool!

GOLDE: Send a postcard, Emma!

(Pause.)

EMMA: Did you hear about Alma?

GOLDE: No, what?

EMMA: She found a place as a servant with Prince Krapotkin. Frau Herta hired her. The German woman.

GOLDE: Thank God! *(To Edit.)* You see? You should look for something like that.

EDIT: I don't know...

GOLDE: This isn't going to last forever.

EDIT: Yes... but...

GOLDE: *(Soothingly.)* We have savings for now. *(To Emma.)* Your father accepts it? *(Emma nods.)* Who will take charge of the butter?

EMMA: Flora, the youngest.

GOLDE: She is how old...?

EMMA: Eleven.

GOLDE: And she can already churn butter?

EMMA: She has very strong arms. She's just afraid of the elves. She says that they sour the milk and the butter. Flora says she wants to go to Argentina when she's older.

GOLDE: We shall see.

EDIT: She's so little...

EMMA: Schlomo says that in Argentina they call boys "*pibe*" or "*pebete*." And a girl, "*papusa*, or *mina*." If she's a poor girl, "*percanta*." And the French women, "*franchutas*." "*Franchutas*," what a word.

(Edit and Golde laugh.)

GOLDE: Is that how the Argentines talk? That's their language?

EMMA: Something like that. It's a kind of Yiddish of theirs.

EDIT: Yiddish!

EMMA: *(Enthusiastically.)* When a man has no money, they say he is "*misho.*" Poverty is "*mishiadura.*" The rich man is called a "*bacán.*" And the fool, "*otario.*" He who is very foolish, "*gil.*" The policeman is called a "button," I don't know why. A ring is called a "*zarzo.*" The home is "*bulín*" or love nest, if there are only two love birds living there. They call the Arabs Turks; the Jews, Russians. Seems like the Argentines don't know much about geography. The place where I'm going is called Rosario. There aren't any Indians in that place anymore, it's a city. He has a little house...

GOLDE: ... painted with lime.

EMMA: He told you?

GOLDE: Yes.

EMMA: With a maid. Housekeeper, he said. Her name is Calista. She cooks empanadas. The empanada is like a turnover. Schlomo says it's very tasty. As soon as I learn to cook it, I'll send the recipe. I'm sure your Moishe will like it.

EDIT: Thank you.

EMMA: The mosquitoes are a plague, he says. But at night it's pretty when there are fireflies. There are many birds. He says the English, who travel a lot, say that nowhere else are there so many birds in such vivid colors as in America. He says he had a friend who had a little owl in her house as a pet. He said a "friend of his" but I think that he was referring to his previous wife. He says that he doesn't have a wife now.

GOLDE: He says he loves you.

EMMA: Yes, he says he loves me. That he fell in love with me as soon as he saw me. He asked me to speak to him as an equal, not to use formal speech, after we are married! A rabbi in Buenos Aires will marry us. Did he tell you that too, Mrs. Golde?

GOLDE: Yes.

EMMA: Do you believe him?

GOLDE: I don't know. Men change wives often; maybe it's true that he wants to marry you because he loves you.

EMMA: *(To all.)* What do you think? Should I believe him or not?

EDIT: Yes.

GOLDE: No.

EDIT: Why not?

GOLDE: He did the same thing to Rut Rosenbaum. Remember Rut? The one who was from the Ukraine? Who came for *Pesach* five years ago? No, no: you were too little, Emma, of course. *(To Edit.)* Your cousin Rudi, daughter, how could you not remember!

EDIT: Yes, yes. I know already. I know the story. He told her that he loved her and he took her away. We don't know if they actually married. Rut couldn't stand that sort of life... Schlomo confessed to Mama that Rut committed suicide.

GOLDE: *(Sad.)* With poison.

EMMA: *(Mortified.)* No!

GOLDE: There is no need for it to happen to you, Emma. You must keep in mind that reality is the true measure of decency.

(A long thoughtful pause.)

EMMA: *(Gloomy.)* Then what? Should I believe Schlomo or should I not believe him?

GOLDE: You can't lose anything by not believing him. What is there to fear? God is on your side. Has God abandoned any of his own? *(Pause.)* Didn't he remove our chains when we were slaves in Egypt? *(Pause. Emma starts to cry very slowly.)* God will also remove your chains, if it comes to it.

EDIT: *(Consoling her.)* Come, come, Emma.

(Emma tries to smile and compose herself.)

GOLDE: Courage.

EDIT: That's better.

GOLDE: Shall we go over what you're going to do?

EMMA: Yes.

GOLDE: It's most likely you'll go ashore in the port of Buenos Aires. If you go ashore in Montevideo, don't lose hope, we'll work out how to help you. What are you going to do then, when you get to the port of Buenos Aires?

EMMA: *(Reciting.)* I'm going to find someone from the Jewish Association for the Protection of Women and Children.

GOLDE: They are in the port, they interview every Jewish woman passenger. They will stop and question you.

EMMA: They will be dressed in black. The men wear a *kippot*.

GOLDE: The women wear gray hats. Some of them are veiled. They will approach you...

EMMA: ... And they will ask why I am going to Argentina. I will tell them that I'm going to get married. They will ask me to whom and how long I have known him. I'm going to tell them the truth, that I'm not sure of anything.

GOLDE: Very well.

EMMA: They will get me out.

GOLDE: Yes.

EMMA: They will take me to a shelter. Then they will return me to Poland.

GOLDE: Yes. *(To Edit.)* Did you see if Moishe is alright?

EMMA: He's better, right? *(Edit and Golde nod, happy. Edit goes behind the screen, brings out a baby in her arms. She sits next to them, uncovers her breast, and feeds him.)* He's a precious baby.

GOLDE: *(Baby-talking, tickling him.)* Isn't he just like his grandma?

EDIT: *(Stern.)* Don't bother him, Mama. Later he won't digest his food well.

GOLDE: *(Serious again.)* But let's return to this other matter. What are you going to do if you don't see anyone from the Association?

EMMA: Nothing.

(Long pause.)

GOLDE: You must have patience Emma: much patience. Maybe Mr. Schlomo loves you, after all. Why not? Maybe he's not lying to us. If he is...

EMMA: I'll write to Bronia Kaufman.

GOLDE: The passwords?

EMMA: I have them embroidered on a petticoat. In code.

GOLDE: Send word to Bronia. And to us. We will do everything we can to rescue you. Berta retired a few months ago. I wrote to her letting her know that you were going. Never trust a madam, a housekeeper. If everything goes wrong... *(Desolate.)* if everything goes wrong, we will be by your side in our hearts. It won't last more than three years, then they'll let you go. It won't last forever. You've climbed out of poverty; you will help your own. Isn't that what matters?

EMMA: I'm going to write to my father every three months... send them some money.

(Golde nods. The three of them get up.)

GOLDE: If we learn that you haven't been able to leave within a year, the next one who goes will take the money to buy your freedom.

EMMA: Who will be next?

GOLDE: *(Looking at Edit.)* I think it will be Rifka Kofman, the blacksmith's daughter.

EMMA: Rifka.

GOLDE: *(Hugs her.)* Goodbye, my dear.

EMMA: Goodbye, Ada.

EDIT: Goodbye, Emma.

EMMA: *(Crying.)* Goodbye.

EDIT: We'll see each other again soon.

(Emma nods and exits.)

GOLDE: *(To Edit.)* Give him to me for a little bit. *(Edit passes her the baby.)* Hello, little baby.

EDIT: How will you do it this time, Mama?

GOLDE: I have it all thought out, Ada. It seems that Mr. Trauman will send me a Romanian this time. Some Jakobson fellow. He doesn't know anything about us. I told him you were a beauty, that your name was Rejzla Kofman. He saw a picture of you. That one with the little cap and the veil...

EDIT: Oh!

GOLDE: You were so pretty there! God has given you the gift of beauty, my daughter. You must be willing to use it on behalf of these pitiful girls...

EDIT: I'm not complaining, Mama.

GOLDE: This Jakobson fellow will come next June. *(Lifting the baby.)* Ohhh. Moishe will be a little elephant by then! A little elephant! Isn't that right, Moishe? Isn't that right? You are going to play a mute.

EDIT: Mute, Mama? Mute?

GOLDE: Mute, Ada. Don't get stubborn with me. It won't be so hard. This time you barely said a word.

EDIT: No... but...

GOLDE: Mr. Jakobson won't want a mute to take to Argentina. This Schlomo fellow already told me: the clients like the women to provide conversation. We will tell him that you are mute from birth, and you have just one sister that your father would be willing to hand over in exchange for a few more rubles: Rifka. Like we did with Emma, and with Sarita, and the others.

EDIT: But Rifka, Mama...

GOLDE: Yes, she's not pretty at all. If we don't do this she'll end up starving to death in the village...

EDIT: And aren't you afraid, Mama, that Mr. Jakobson will prefer some other girl from the village? Anastasia, the little Russian girl, or...

GOLDE: *(Authoritarian.)* Mr. Trauman trusts in my judgment. Who's going to offer him the little Russian girl?

EDIT: *(Tired.)* No one, Mama, I was just saying.

GOLDE: *(Continuing.)* The blacksmith agrees. During the time you pretend to be Rifka's sister you will live with them, and I will stay with my precious *(She makes faces at the baby.)* Móishele.

EDIT: What is Sarita doing these days?

GOLDE: Excuse me?

EDIT: What has Sarita been doing since she came back from Argentina? Where is she?

GOLDE: Sarita? Oh, oh, Sarita Bronstein. She's in Warsaw. Soon she'll move to Berlin.

EDIT: Sarita always had itchy feet...

GOLDE: Yes...

EDIT: Oh, Mama. Don't bounce Moishe like that!

GOLDE: Shh. Be quiet.

(Pause.)

EDIT: There's something I don't like, Mama.

GOLDE: Yes?

EDIT: I had problems this time.

GOLDE: Oh yes? With who?

EDIT: With...

GOLDE: With Mr. Schlomo? Did he make a pass? Yes? Was it when he went to see you on the hillside? Pig! *(Pause.)* What? Ada! Won't you tell me?

EDIT: No, Mama. It wasn't Mr. Schlomo.

GOLDE: No? Then who?

EDIT: Emma's father.

GOLDE: Pan Volf! Did he touch you?

EDIT: Yes, Mama.

GOLDE: And what else?

EDIT: Nothing else.

GOLDE: What do you mean nothing else?

EDIT: I stopped him. I told him that he can only conceive female children and that if he touched me he would make a girl child, that he knows then how difficult it is to settle girl children, that you have to hand them over like sheep to the slaughter...

GOLDE: *(Incredulous.)* And that stopped him?

EDIT: He was drunk on vodka. He threw himself at my feet, he tore his clothing and started to cry. "I'm a bastard!" he shouted. *(Changing her tone.)* That's enough swinging him around like that, Mama. Give me Moishe. *(Her mother hands him over. Edit plays with the baby, she lifts him in the air and rocks him.)* He is precious, isn't he?

(Golde contemplates the baby, she caresses him, and slowly draws out her words.)

GOLDE: Poor bastard.

(Blackout.)

THE GIRLS FROM THE 3.5 FLOPPIES

LUIS ENRIQUE GUTIÉRREZ ORTIZ MONASTERIO

translated by
ANA ELENA PUGA

Left to right: Aída López and Gabriela Murray, in *The Girls from the 3.5 Floppies*, Teatro Principal de la Ciudad de Puebla, Mexico, on November 23, 2007. Photo by Javier B. Camacho Martínez. Courtesy of Javier B. Camacho Martínez.

Translator's Note: Sometimes a Chayote Is Not a Vegetable

One of the challenges in translating LEGOM's *Girls* is its bawdiness and political incorrectness. What to do with words like "*chango*," "*chocho*," "*chayote*," and "*modorro*," which in the context of the play sound hilarious in Spanish when used to refer to female genitalia but which literally translated into English refer to a monkey, cinnamon candy, a green vegetable, and a sleepy or stupid person? What to do with one character's sensible advice to the other that she get herself a "*verga de planta*"? A permanent penis? A house dick? And what to do with the characters' unattractive tendency to refer to their gay acquaintances as "*maricones*" (literally, "fags")? Not to mention the stereotypical reference to the supposed lack of sexual endowment of Japanese men. Do I edit and clean up the language lest readers accuse LEGOM of stereotyping and homophobia, or do I resist the urge to sanitize and instead reproduce passages that might produce a wince instead of a laugh from some spectators? Though I chose to keep most of the potentially offensive language, I did decide that under certain circumstances "*maricón*" has lost its original reference to sexual orientation and has acquired a more neutral offensive connotation (if neutral offensiveness is possible), similar to how "bastard" no longer refers to the children of unwed parents and "asshole" does not usually refer to human anatomy. Moreover, the meaning of the term can differ according to the context. "*Maricón*" thus became "boy toy" in one instance and "gasbag" in another.

Ana Elena Puga

The Girls from the 3.5 Floppies [*Las chicas del tres y media floppies*] premiered on August 6, 2004 at DramaFest in Mexico City, directed by John Tiffany.

CAST   Aída López
                                  Gabriela Murray

In 2008, the play toured to El Centro Su Teatro, Denver (February 11-17); the Museum of Contemporary Art, Chicago (February 18-23); and 7 Stages, Atlanta (February 24-March 1) with the same cast and director.

SCENIC DESIGN   Juliana Faesler
LIGHTING   Martha Ladrón de Guevara
COSTUMES   Bertha Romero
SOUND DESIGN   Alejandra Hernández
SUPERTITLE TRANSLATION   Tatiana Lipkes

This translation is based on an unpublished manuscript emailed by the author. A slightly different Spanish-language version of the play was published in *Dramaturgia Mexicana hoy,* eds. Jorge Dubatti and Luis Mario Moncada. (Buenos Aires: Editorial Atuel and Mexico, DF: CONACULTA, Centro Cultural Helénico, 2005) 83-109. At the request of the author, the punctuation from the original Spanish, with its scarcity of commas and question marks, was maintained in this English version.

1

Got some coke?

No.

Have you seen Loser?

Who is Loser?

The guy who got your cousin pregnant, who else.

Is Joya pregnant?

Of course not. But he did get her pregnant.

I didn't know.

Well Loser told me that he stayed here last night.

Oh, that moron.

And he told me that you've still got coke.

If I still had some, your Loser wouldn't have gone off with my can opener at five in the morning.

He had something to do. I think he sends his apologies.

He can stick them where the sun don't shine.

He says you've still got coke.

Who does that jerk think he is giving out inventories of my apartment?

Do you or do you not have some?

You're a pain in the ass.

I'll pay you for it.

Can't you see I'm busy?

It's good to be busy with something.

Yes.

Yes.

Well yes.

Know anyone who might have some coke?

Didn't you say you had money?

So?

Go look for some and stop bugging me.

Tomorrow's the deadline for the school payment.

Then you don't have any.

I do, but it's like I don't.

Then you don't.

I'm going to talk to the principal. I'm going to tell her the one about the gynecologist. You know, that I had some tests done and I can't walk much.

That's an old one. All the mothers blow the registration fees on pills and liquor and then go to the principal with the business about the gynecologist. She's not going to swallow it.

Not all the mothers.

All the ones I know.

You don't know many.

I know all the fucking mothers in the world. Mothers who never have money to pay the school and come to ask me: Got any coke? Got any coke? I've got money, but it's for the school. Got any coke?

Don't mimic me.

Whatever you say.

Joaquín's moved into second grade now.

So what?

He's in the same grade as your kid now.

Mine's moved into third grade. The girl is in first. So they're not in the same year and God forbid they ever be in the same class so I don't end up in the same parent-teacher conference next to you, and you'll be nagging about the coke thing while the teacher asks us to give the kids twenty pesos to take them to the theater.

How do you know all that about the meetings?

Because Salvador tells me about them.

And you talk to him now?

We never stopped talking.

Before you would rip each other a new one if you ran into each other at the 3.5, and now it turns out that you never stopped talking.

That's none of your business.

Do you still fuck?

That's also none of your business.

Do you fuck or not?

...

...

Sometimes, at the end of the month.

He gives you money?

I ask him for a food allowance.

But he's got the kids.

And what do you think I eat, dummy? Seaweed?

He's not obligated to by law.

And I'm not obligated by law to talk to you, but I talk, because I am a good person, just like Salvador, who without being obligated by law gives me money for food. Of course, even if a judge ordered Salvador to talk to you he'd rather be sent to the María Islands as a free bitch for the convicts.

If you don't want to fuck he doesn't give you money?

Who comes up with your questions? You by yourself, or does that Loser guy help you? Hey didn't you hear what I said to you?

If you don't want to fuck he doesn't give you money?

I always want to fuck and he always wants to pay for my groceries. Does that answer your question?

What if one day at the end of the month you didn't want to fuck because your pussy was broken or because they had slashed your muffin up the middle during a fight in front of the 3.5 Floppies, then do you think he would give you money?

Where do you get so much bullshit from?

They cut open Lola's muff in front of the 3.5 Floppies. They said it's going to be twice as long.

Poor thing.

In the VGA bar she ran into that woman who had stolen her city ID. She pulled her out by the hair, but you know. There are irresponsible people, with knives and everything. Her melting pot is going to be twice as long.

At least now those two fists she'd dreamed of will fit in there.

You remember? How funny.

Yes, how funny, move, I need to get by.

So? Would he give you the money?

Who?

Salvador. If you don't put out for him.

I think so. But that's none of your business.

You really don't have any?

Do you want a Prozac?

At least.

If I give you a Prozac will you get off my back?

It would be better if you had four.

Take them all.

Are you cured already?

Prozac isn't to cure me, it's to cure everything around me, I would take it and the world would lift its head and smile, but it doesn't seem to work anymore. Wherever I turn, everything is sad. Seems like not even Prozac will cure it.

Do you think that if I find him, even if I don't want to fuck, he might lend me something for the school?

Could you repeat that?

What?

What you said earlier.

The thing about Prozac?

The thing about Salvador.

Oh, the thing about Salvador. That.

That.

Well, well I am asking if he could lend me money to pay the school even if I don't want to give him a piece of ass.

I don't think so.

Didn't you say he was a nice guy?

But he's not your piggy bank, dummy.

Changing, changing, changing, changing the question. Do you think he could lend me something for the school?

If you give him a piece of ass.

Well, if it's necessary.

So why don't you go offer yourself to the father of your kid and leave the father of mine alone?

I offered already. He's broke. His mother came to live with him and she's more expensive than a Jaguar with a broken fuel pump.

Jaguars don't have fuel pumps.

How do you know?

I don't know but if you say it, you must be wrong. And besides the comparison is very idiotic.

Well his old lady is living with him and she's more expensive than an idiot ex-girlfriend.

That's better.

That's how he put it to me. More expensive than an idiot ex-girlfriend.

Think it might be because of you?

Because of me, why? No, I don't think so. The thing is the old lady plays bingo at Crayfish Plaza. Don't you know her? She's got a mustache and she goes along the shore with an enormous Calvin Klein bag. She spends about twenty dollars a day on bingo and drinks more than a dozen of those soft drinks they give you while you play. Oh, sure, but she hangs up the phone on me when I want to talk to him.

Asshole bitch.

She says she doesn't have any grandchildren. And she hangs up on me.

Take her the kid, like my sister. Her ex-husband wouldn't even give her a safety pin, she went and threw the kid at his grandparents. It was about eleven o'clock at night. The next day they brought him back with an envelope full of bills and coins. About five hundred dollars.

She took them?

The kid, not in your dreams. She took the envelope and slammed the door on their false teeth. "So you can see what a pain in the ass it is to raise a kid, damn indigent old farts."

Are they indigent?

It's an insult. She wanted to call them miserly but she couldn't remember the word. It happens.

The indigent part is good anyway. Well, I need the school money.

Didn't you say you had it already?

Yes, but if I do a few lines of caine, which I think I will, I'm going to end up owing my Joaquincito everything up to and including college.

Well go watch some TV dramas and don't spend the money.

Does Salvador also pay for the kids' school?

I hope so.

Where is he living now?

No, dummy. I don't think you understood that that guy is off-limits.

I was just asking.

Well I'm just answering you.

You don't want to go out?

No.

Are you going to stay cooped up in this heat?

Look, if what you want is to go to the 3.5 Floppies to score a gram of powder, go for it.

Have I talked to you about my friend Fermincito, the sculptor?

About twenty times.

Well he introduced me to some gentlemen from Tijuana.

The people you're getting mixed up with. It's going to end badly.

They're not what you think. They have a business where you place bets. It's in Tijuana. We got along good. They thought it was very funny that my mother-in-law blew the child support for the kid on bingo. You get it? Because they live off of the money those old ladies pay them.

I got it.

One of them has a tarantula in a fish bowl.

And does the fish bowl have water in it?

No, the spider would drown.

Then what is so extraordinary about that.

The spider is called Thirst.

Out of the ordinary.

Right? They told me to call them. That if I take some friends we can go dancing at their house.

And?

I'll call them.

Didn't they say some friends?

No, well, yes. But let's both go and tell them that Lola couldn't come because they are patching up her milk dud.

And will they have enough to pay up?

They're loaded.

I'll think about it.

What's there to think about?

That that's how Coral started and she just got five years in McAllen.

These guys are different. They even have yachts.

And how does that make them different?

They have yachts.

You are the most moronic moron I have ever met.

If you say so. Want me to call them?

They cut off the telephone.

Do you still have the card I lent you the other day?

It ran out.

It doesn't matter, I know a trick. I just need the card.

What is the trick.

I won't tell you because then you'll do it too.

Then I won't lend it to you.

Well, we're not going anywhere.

I'm not the one going around like a pregnant bitch looking for a line of coke to pop out her seven pups. I was just fine fixing up my home until you arrived.

Seriously?

...

OK. But don't tell Carla. You stick the card in and you call an 800 number they gave me. When the operator answers you put in the other numbers they gave me and you make a free call.

Where is the phone number from?

I think it's from Mexico City.

You're going to make a long-distance call through an operator in order to end up making a local call?

Yes. More or less.

Does that seem right?

What, are you paying for it?

Doesn't it seem illogical?

No. Teach a lesson to the guy who put in the 800 number.

You seriously think that?

Yes.

You have a code that lets you talk for free to anywhere in the world and you use it to make local calls?

If you want to see it that way.

You only use it to make local calls?

I don't know anyone outside of here.

Your world is so small.

Yes, looks like it. Sometimes I look at it and it seems far away, very far away, but it's not far, it's small.

And you who love to dance with people from outer space, hasn't it ever occurred to you to ask them for their phone number?

Like for what?

To call them with your little card, dummy, what else for.

And what would I say to them?

Whatever you want. Just call them.

Well, it could be a good excuse to ask them their names. You know, "listen, write down your phone number so I can call you sometime. I never lose track of my friends. Never."

Look, see how easily that came out. To hook you don't have to go to Harvard or Gomorrah.

And if they don't speak Spanish?

And if they don't speak Spanish. And if they don't speak Spanish. Well then you're screwed.

I can learn languages.

You? In five years here all you've learned is that "tu foquen dic, machote."

You taught me that.

Thank you.

You've taught me a lot of what I know.

Thank you.

I could also call my mother.

If you don't have anything to say to a German who stuffed it in my chiquis triquis, what are you going to have to talk about with your mother.

That's true. That's true.

Sorry, I didn't mean to say that.

No, it's alright. It's alright.

No, I didn't mean to say that. I wouldn't know what to talk about with mine either, supposing she had something to tell me. How long has it been since you've seen her?

About seven years. Listen, maybe my mother will lend us the school money. I'll tell her to deposit it tomorrow and we can go stock up on coke.

And if she says no?

It doesn't matter, we'll stock up the pantry anyway.

And how are you going to pay the kid's school?

If she tells me no, it means yes. The old lady is sort of contradictory, but she has a good heart.

You mean she's a moron.

I mean that she wouldn't let her grandson drop out of school.

Does she already know that she has a grandson?

She'll find out now.

Isn't that too much news all at once?

It seems like a lot to you?

You tell her where you live, that you have a son and that you need her to deposit the school money because you're going to get stoned up to your ears in coke tonight. Doesn't that seem like a lot?

I'm not going to tell her the part about the coke.

And she won't know.

That's her problem.

What does she know about you?

I tell you we haven't talked that much.

Does she think you're still living with that worthless shit?

I guess. Though she knows I never last a year.

I don't think she's likely to slip you anything. And know what else, I bet she's going to want to hop on the first Federal Express plane to meet her grandson.

Ha. Gotcha. FedEx doesn't carry people.

And who says your lump of a mom is a person?

You don't even know her.

The Federal Express thing was an expression. Tomorrow you'll have her here and she'll stay dug in for a week.

You think?

That's how they are.

I don't care. If she comes, we can re-establish our relationship.

Where did you read that about "re-establishing relationships"?

I think it was in *Beach Today*. In an article about Tibet.

Since when do you read newspapers?

I don't know. Whenever I can. They leave them in the hotels. In the morning I read the newspaper and watch *Sponge Bob*. Sometimes I go out to the balcony and watch the waves. It's fucking great to see the waves from the tenth floor. I say to myself: "Look how high up you've climbed, who would have thought it."

And yes, who would have thought it.

Shall I call my mom?

If you want, but whatever you do, don't bring her by here at eleven to ask me if I have coke.

My mom is a decent person.

Whatever you say. We'd dropped it.

No. We were talking about re-establishing relationships. We all need a mother.

I don't.

I need my mother.

And after seven years you come to realize this?

I can patch things up with her. I'll take her out with her grandson for a few days and then I'll get her to commit to a monthly allowance for school fees and things like that.

Hey, I'm going to call mine too.

Finally, you pay attention to me.

I was joking.

Sure, since you have... since you have your... Where did you tell me Salvador lives?

I didn't tell you where he lives, I didn't give you his number, I'm not going to let you get near him and the only person who he gives money to and who he's going to keep giving it to at the end of the month, is to me.

You've never asked him for anything in-between the end of the month?

It's called before the end of the month and no, he has never given me anything before the end of the month because I haven't asked him for it.

Why don't you call him?

Because I don't need money, that's why.

But I do.

Well that's why.

Tell him it's an emergency.

Why don't you take the Prozac already and let me finish this up.

Do you want me to help you?

Do you know how to iron?

No, but I'll help you.

Do you know how to vacuum?

No, but I'll help you.

You're not going to climb very high like that.

Higher than the tenth floor?

Look, the only chance you have of surviving, assuming you don't die or get locked up in McAllen, is getting yourself a permanent dick. One who concerns himself with you, with your son, and with keeping you away from that witch of a mother of yours. And to get yourself a house-dick you have to have certain homemaking skills, besides making ferocious noises when they move it around inside you. So there.

You're an enterprising woman. Do you know that they are going to open a café in the 3.5 Floppies?

The Cyberbitches. I already knew it. And what's that got to do with anything?

I guess I'm not as bright as you.

No, I think not. Listen, please. You go home. You're not going to call either your mother or those thugs from Tijuana, you are not going to go to the 3.5 Floppies to get hooked up. Tomorrow, at the crack of dawn you pay the goddamn school and you learn to do something decent with your life and you let me do something decent with mine.

Oh, that's why you don't want to go with my friends from Tijuana.

Are you listening to me?

That's why you're cleaning everything. You want to learn to be a homemaker mom and all that stuff.

No, I am cleaning up my habitat because I don't like it to be a pigsty like yours, that's why.

And why today in particular? You never clean.

Because I'm fed up with certain things. That's why.

Are you expecting anyone?

No.

Loser told me that you invited him to come over whenever he wants.

Your goddamn Loser ran off with my can opener at dawn. I didn't know they called him Loser and I don't care what they call him at the police station either. I didn't invite him to come in and I didn't invite him to plop himself down here like it was his home.

He told me that he's thinking of coming to live with you. That you agreed to split the rent.

He must have dreamed it, because if I see him again, I won't even recognize him, and if I do recognize him I'm just going to curse him out for my electric can opener.

Then he's not going to live here.

Do I have to tell you again?

No, I got it already. Then why are you cleaning up the place?

Goddamn it with you.

OK, OK. Listen, I thought the room would be taken. I know, I know that the Loser thing didn't work out, but I thought it had, that's why I hadn't asked about the room.

What do you want to know about the room?

I owe four months rent.

Like the four months you owed when I threw you out for not paying your share.

It wasn't because my Joaquincito peed on your bathing suits?

That was the last straw but you owed the rent. The room is still available but not for you or for that fartface.

Just while I get another one.

Like the last time.

I think they're going to throw me out.

Why don't you ask your mom for the rent too?

Didn't you say I shouldn't call her?

As far as I'm concerned, call whoever you like, but you're not moving into the
room.

I'll pay you the months I still owe.

But when I asked you for it, you threw a glass of water in my face. Have you
forgotten that?

Seriously?

You don't remember?

No, when was it?

Six months ago in the 3.5 Floppies.

Oh, when I was playing pool with those French guys.

In the Plugandplay room.

Yes, of course, with the French guys. What must they have thought of me.

You're right. You know how some people are malicious.

Really?

I don't want it to seem like I'm kicking you out, but why don't you fuck off. I'm
expecting company.

Oh, weren't you cleaning to change your life?

What I do with my life should be as unimportant to you as what you do with
your ass is to me. Could you leave?

If you ask me to.

If you want me to I'll ask.

Are you sure you don't have any coke left?

Are you leaving?

I'll look for you later. I have to go call my mother.

2

Joaquín, Joaquín.

You don't have to yell.

That damn kid ran off on me again. Listen, don't you have some coke?

I don't have any.

Would you give me a little bit?

No.

Got some or not?

No.

Do you know where Joaquín is?

I haven't seen him.

What time did you get in yesterday?

What's it to you?

I was just asking. Listen, when does that guy in your bed plan on leaving?

Is he bothering you?

No, I was just asking.

He left a while ago.

He went out to the balcony to puke, but he went back in to sleep.

And afterwards I asked him to leave.

And who is he?

I don't know. I met him in the Chat Room Danger.

You went to the 3.5 Floppies and you didn't invite me?

You weren't here.

You could have left me a message. I had a shitty time.

Where were you?

With the boat guys.

What a drag.

You're telling me.

They started to hit on each other.

Like always.

Weren't you looking for Joaquín?

Where is he?

I don't know, I'm just asking. You wake me up screaming and then you forget about him.

So you went to the 3.5 Floppies. Did you see him?

Who.

You know.

Yes, he was there.

And what did he say to you?

Nothing. I don't speak to him.

They were supposed to make him a captain.

When did he tell you this?

He came to see Joaquín.

Well when I saw him he was a waiter.

He wasn't wearing the CD-ROM apron?

No.

The one from Mouse.

I didn't notice.

Then how do you know he wasn't wearing the CD-ROM apron?

I didn't notice him and there is nothing to see in him, but if he had been wearing the fucking CD-ROM apron I would have noticed because finally in his life, there would have been something to notice about him. OK?

OK. He told me it was a done deal.

And what if they do promote him?

It's good for him and good for us. Shall I make you a coffee?

I made it already.

Can I get some?

No, you haven't bought any.

Just a little bit?

Alright.

Who knows what those damn boat guys gave me to drink. Do you know that they are going to start charging women in the 3.5 Floppies?

They've always charged.

But now we're not going to get the complimentary happy-hour-broadband-access buffet if we go with a dick. Now they're going to charge for drinks.

The place is going to empty out on them.

And those prices. The Lotus 1-2-3 with vodka, four dollars. And the Multimedia Drunk, six.

How do you know the prices?

You don't listen to me, didn't I tell you that he came to see Joaquín? He bought him some shoes.

Wow, he's finally taking responsibility.

But they didn't fit him. And I think he bought them at a second-hand place. He said he was going to bring some new ones, but he hasn't come back. And what's up with you?

With what?

You haven't seen your kids?

What do you want me to see in them?

I don't know, whatever mothers see in them. The eyes, for instance. Some check out their backside, others pay a lot of attention to their hairstyle. I don't know.

Well not me. Did they tell you that the Arabs are going to give a wet t-shirt party?

Yes, on Thursday.

Are you going?

I have to take care of Joaquín.

Leave him with his dad.

He works Thursdays.

So, he can take him to work with him.

That jerk? Don't you believe it. Did I tell you that the other day I went to look for him so that he would sign the maternity papers? It was noon already and he wouldn't pay any attention to me. I was fed up to here because I had the kid, I had left him in the Microballs game room, no cruising there, but they had already invited me to a thong party for the Superbowl and I was going to set it up with the little blond boy toy from the other day. Isn't it reasonable for him to lend me the telephone so that I could let the blond boy toy know that I was running late, that he should pick me up at the 3.5? Well no. "Telephone use is restricted to paying customers." It's a public utility, asshole. No fucking way. "Well, I'm going now, I'll leave your son here and you figure it out." Would you believe that he called the Antivirus Squad to throw me out together with Joaquín? No, I don't think that jerk is going to want to watch him.

It's your loss. You never get to go to the Arabs' parties.

I'm tired of this. I'm going to call my mother. This week. I'm going to tell her that I'm moving back in with her.

And Joaquín?

He can stay with his father a while. That little brat makes my life a nightmare. I can't get a dick because he's always looking for a way to run them off. I'm going back to my mom, without the kid. I'm going to get myself a guy, and once he's stuck on me I'll tell him about Joaquín to see what kind of face he makes.

What time is it?

You're not listening to me.

I have an appointment in half an hour, if you want to put in the complaint that your life is shit, write it down on a sticky note and I'll read it later.

Where are you going?

They invited me to lunch.

The guy who was puking a while ago?

No, a friend of his who is leaving for Laredo tomorrow. Listen, let me know if you decide to leave so that I can find someone to take your room.

I'll let you know. Let me talk to my mom. Now let me see where I left her phone number. I had it written down on a napkin.

You should buy yourself a phonebook.

I'm going to do that.

So you don't lose so much stuff.

3

Let me see that eye.

Got any coke?

It's getting better. Did you go to the dentist?

I'm going this week, he's going to put in some plastic ones.

How much will it cost you?

No idea.

You're going to have a scar on your eye.

Got any coke?

You haven't finished bringing in your crap and you're already nagging about the coke. Don't you have anyone else to ask?

No, and I'm done. That's all I've got.

That's all.

Yes.

What have you got in that box?

My belongings.

And the rest?

Everything fits in here.

Everything you have fits in one box?

More or less. And the bag of clothes.

You're almost forty years old and everything you've done in life fits in one box?

Yeah, not much, huh?

No, doesn't look like it. What's this?

Leave it, it's my life insurance.

It's fucked up that you put your whole life in a single box, but that the only thing you have in that box is Bibles, that's pathetic. What do you want them for?

I'm telling you, they're my life insurance.

Where did you get them?

Where else from, the hotels.

Didn't you say you read *Beach Today*?

I read it, but it's worthless, the Bibles I bring with me.

And you steal the fucking blue Bibles from the motels?

And what did you want?

Didn't you ever think it might be better to take the towels or the little shampoos? For example.

I do take the shampoos, but I've finished them all by now. The towels don't fit in my bag.

You should use a bigger bag.

Yes, I've thought about it. Then I could take the sheets too.

Oh, you poor thing. And since when have you been taking the Bibles?

Since always.

I don't remember you having any Bible when you lived here.

And I don't remember Salvador coming at the end of the month to get a little pussy in exchange for some dough.

And what the hell do you want the Bibles for.

I can sell them in case I get into a tight spot.

You're always in a tight spot. For example, now. Why do you think you haven't sold them?

No, no. A real tight spot. Suppose I'm dying.

You're not getting it. Who do you think would be interested in a thousand motel Bibles?

Three hundred forty seven.

However many. Who?

Someone who likes reading the Bible more than *Beach Today*?

Someone who likes reading the Bible more than *Beach Today* is not going to buy Gideon Bibles.

Which ones are those?

The ones you've got there, with the blue covers, are the Gideons.

Seriously? I've never opened them.

People who are interested in Bibles buy the Latin American Edition, not Gideon. They give away the Gideon version in motels because if they didn't give it away no one would open it.

Then you don't think I'll be able to sell them?

Don't even lug them around, leave them at the entrance so the garbage men take them away.

Oh no. How can you think that I would throw a Bible in the garbage.

It's a sin, right?

Don't make fun of my religions, or you'll burn in Hell. Do you or do you not have coke?

...

They say that the old lady from the Desseperatio lost an eye because she went around blaspheming.

That one-eyed lady lost an eye because she tried to stick it in where it doesn't belong. Don't be superstitious.

I'm a believer, which is not the same. People who believe in God and things like that are believers, and people who don't believe in God but are afraid of him are superstitious, in other words, the nonbelievers.

What do you know! Who said dummies can't practice theology.

Well I'm not going to throw away the blessed Holy Bibles.

Gideon version.

Whatever version it is. I'm going to start reading them all beginning today. All of them.

All the Bibles?

All the ones I have here.

But they all say the same thing.

They're not like the *Beach Today*?

The *Beach Today* is about things that are happening on this beach, and even if nothing happens, each thing that doesn't happen changes from week to week. The Bible is about matters of eternity, and eternity happened long before a gringo gasbag decided to edit a newspaper for tourists, and since God has more words than a gringo gasbag, the Bible says the same thing and *Beach Today* contradicts itself every week. Got it?

That's what you think because you don't know anything about God or the angels.

Do what you want. And Joaquincito?

He's not with me.

Where is he.

I listened to you. I dumped him with his grandparents. Teach them a lesson. In two weeks they'll be wanting to return him. But this time I'm not taking back diddly-squat.

If you don't have Joaquín anymore, then why were you bugging me about the room.

For me to live in, dummy.

You don't need a home. You don't even have a mattress. Do you have the rent?

I wanted to talk to you about that. Do you remember the twins who danced with the boa at the Alligator?

Have you got the rent?

Will you let me finish talking?

When you pay me.

First listen to me, OK?

I'm listening.

Do you remember the identical twins who danced with the boa at the Alligator?

You asked me that already.

Do you remember or not?

Yes, what's up with them.

Well they're not twins anymore, because the one with the mole on her tit died.

They're still twins, one alive and the other dead.

Then they're not identical twins anymore, at most they're fraternal. The point is that they fucked her up.

Don't you dare tell me that the boa strangled her because you'll get out with your fucking Bibles and all and go pray on street corners.

Let me finish. They went out on a yacht with the boa. Some Japanese guys hired her. You know how the Japanese have real little thingy-wingies, so if she could stick half a boa up her papaya, it was no problem to dance for the little Japanese guys.

The point.

In mid-show the boa fell into the sea.

You're shitting me.

Yes. And the one with the mole on her left tit dove into the water after it. And she didn't know how to swim.

And the Japanese?

The Japanese? They were up to their eyeballs in dope and tequila. You think they were going to get her out? They clapped for her. Imagine how awful it must be to be drowning while twelve Japanese guys in Hawaiian shirts clap for you from the bow. The other twin only managed to fish out the boa. Looks like she's going to recover.

It must be awful to drown.

The propeller passed over her head and turned it to shit before she drowned.

Well, in that case she was lucky.

She sure was. At least she didn't drown or burn.

And what does this have to do with the rent?

Let me finish. Fermincito told me about this.

You found the sculptor?

Yes. He told me he was going to get some hash.

You gave my rent money to Fermincito so he could buy hash?

Yes, but he didn't come back. He gets it really cheap. We can re-sell it.

What the fuck are you going to re-sell if he fucked off with the money, dingbat.

No, he wouldn't do something like that to me.

You want me to believe that bullshit about the twins and the boa and the hash?

If you want, ask. They're burying her tomorrow.

Tell it to your mom.

Well, too bad for you.

No, too bad for you because you don't come in here with your things until you pay me.

Wait. Wait. We can settle the rent. I'll leave you the Bibles as collateral.

Gosh, why didn't I think of that?

I know you don't believe in God and all that crap but don't let that influence you.

No, it's not that I don't believe in God, supposing that God wants someone to believe in Him. What I don't believe in is in the value of your damn Bibles.

You see what I mean.

I see what, dimwit.

It is better to believe in God.

I used to think you were playing dumb, now I know it's true.

You know what I told Fermincito? That I can count on you. I told him that you are better than my mother. If one day I have problems.

You're going to sell the Bibles.

No, problems, problems so big that people wouldn't understand, problems so big that not even selling the Bibles would save me from them. Evolutionary issues.

What's that about evolutionary issues?

I told you already, big ones. Issues that are big even for God, evolutionary issues, the kind that even God doesn't know how to solve.

You are an evolutionary issue.

We are all an evolutionary issue, an issue for God. If I get into one of those specific evolutionary issues, I am going to come to you and you are going to save me.

Warn me so that I don't open the door.

Thanks. I knew I could count on you.

That doesn't solve the rent thing. Look, Salvador couldn't lend me anything this month and I need to pay the landlady.

With my money.

With your deposit, like we agreed, which is a fraction of what I left that toothless woman, that's what I'm going to pay her with, not your money.

Why did you say that about toothless?

The landlady is missing some teeth.

You said it because of me.

I didn't say it because of you. I just said that I am going to pay this month with what you give for your part of the deposit. Not with your money.

Well, you're right because you aren't going to get my money. I told you, Fermincito took it and I haven't seen him. Can I stay?

If you want, tomorrow she'll throw us both out.

I won't let that happen.

You make me feel so much better.

...

...

...

...

What do we do?

Call your friends from Tijuana.

Are you sure? Sometimes they get kind of violent.

What do we have to lose.

I didn't want to see them anymore. Let's go to the 3.5 Floppies instead, something will come up.

We need cash, not lines.

It scares me. Last time...

Well call your mom.

I already called her the other day.

And what happened?

I think she doesn't live there anymore.

You think?

A man answered the phone, very angry, because it was three in the morning, you know, the usual. And since he was yelling at me I didn't get the part about my mom very well.

What didn't you understand?

That. Whether she moved, or she died.

He told you that she died?

I told you, I didn't understand.

Well you should have called again. That's important.

People move often. And especially my mother. Ever since she had a fight with the guy from the hairstylist for fags.

But people don't die that often. That was important.

You think?

Yes. Let's call again.

What you want is for me to ask her for help with the rent.

Goddamn it. I want to know if your mom died.

And why do you care so much?

Because it's not right for people to die.

I tell you, you should read the Bible more.

Where is the number?

In my phonebook.

Give it to me.

But I haven't told you what happened with the guys from Tijuana.

What does that have to do with your dead mom?

That I lost the phonebook. That's what. I think I left it at their place. Anyway, it doesn't matter because my mom doesn't live there anymore, I'm telling you I think she moved or something like that.

Well let's call your friends from Tijuana to ask for the phonebook.

And if we call them, then why do we need to ask my mom for money?

I really don't want to ask her for anything.

Anyway, I had the phone number of the guys from Tijuana in the phonebook. So we can't call them.

How did you lose the phonebook? And what are you going to do now?

Nothing, it just had those two numbers.

Just those two? That's what you want a phonebook for?

What else for.

Because you're talking about your mother's phone number and the one for the guys in Tijuana, and when you talk about them and say that they were in your phonebook, it seems like you have a lot more numbers in there.

Why? I told you already that I never ask tourists for their numbers.

Because everything we do represents something more, dummy.

No, not for me. Whatever I figure out right off about someone, that's enough. What do I want to fill the phonebook with numbers for?

What an idiot!

You don't think you're making a big deal out of a phonebook?

Forget about it. How do we find your friends in Tijuana.

I'm telling you I don't want to go with them. Seriously.

Do you know how to find them?

Yes, but I don't want to, OK?

Well we have no choice.

They had this prick tied to a chair.

What are you talking about?

When I went with your friend. Afterwards I went to look for them. The ones from Tijuana.

And they had someone tied up?

Yes, a guy.

Who was he?

How should I know, they had lifted the skin off his face.

And why didn't you tell me this?

Because you wouldn't let me move in if I told you.

How could I leave you on your own.

A while ago you were going to throw me out because I didn't have the rent.

And what did you do?

I ran out, but I was so scared that I split my lip against the arm of a damn Venus de Milo in the garden. And that's where I lost my phonebook and my two teeth.

That's not what you told me before.

I was scared.

Did they chase you?

No, they had even told me to come in. I tell you, they like me a lot.

And why did you leave?

I got scared.

Then there's no problem with them?

I don't know. Maybe not.

Well we should figure out the rent business.

You seriously want us to go?

You say they're your friends. What's the problem.

I don't want to go. What if this time we're jinxed?

Well we have no choice, my dear.

Alright. But I told you so.

Let's go.

Hey, if they ask, you're a rug muncher. When they told me to invite my friends, they specified: "But they should be rug munchers."

What's up with that?

I think they like them.

Alright. I'll say I'm a rug muncher.

Listen, the bright side is that if something happens to us we won't leave our children alone.

That's a plus.

You saw what happened with the twin. She left behind three kids.

But her sister's still here.

That's true. And the boa.

Shouldn't we make ourselves up before going?

I'm fine like this.

Then let's go.

Hey, don't you have a little bit of coke left somewhere, for the road?

In my room, inside the Fátima.

You shouldn't store those things inside the Virgin.

What's wrong with that, she's made of plaster, it won't hurt her.

You know what I think, that maybe we don't represent anything.

What?

You said we represent something. But I think we don't represent shit. Even if people want to see more telephone numbers in us, we're like my phonebook, only what we've filled in, and that's almost nothing.

We're worth dick.

Pure fucking dick.

Or less. Not like the people you say mean nothing but mean a lot. Where do I set it up?

Use the glass on the diploma that's on top of the cat-bank.

Is it Japanese?

I don't think so.

Well it looks it.

Did you find the diploma already?

You studied data entry? That's awesome.

Get used to it.

Later you can show me how to use a computer.

You know, I didn't learn much.

Have I told you that I love you?

Yes, many times, many times.

Let's go, it's far.

Let's go.

What did you think of that stuff about us not representing anything?

What.

That stuff about being only what we can see of ourselves. What did you think?

It's good. It doesn't even seem like it's yours.

Right? You see that I'm not such a moron?

No, you don't even represent that. Let's go now. And later we'll look for your mom, to see if she left you an inheritance.

4

Got some coke?

No. Fuck off.

Hey, your apartment's pretty.

There's a spare room, if you're interested.

Seriously?

Why do you always ask if what I tell you is serious?

It looks good. How much does it rent for?

Four hundred.

Seriously, you don't have any coke?

Again.

They told me you had some.

They told you wrong.

What are you going to do today?

I'm going to the 3.5 Floppies.

You hook up fast. Can I go with you?

I don't think they'll let you in. You're not cool enough.

I'll change quickly.

I wasn't talking about your clothes.

Just so you know, I'm there all the time.

And why haven't I ever seen you?

Maybe it's because you spend your time hooking in the Chat Room Danger?

Whatever you say.

If I bring you the money tomorrow, when can I move in?

I have to tell the landlady so she takes all this junk away.

It's not yours?

No, it was there already when I moved in.

Does it belong to the landlady?

How can you ask such dumb questions? It belongs to the girls who were renting the apartment before. Don't touch anything.

It's not a lot of things. I can move in, there's room for me anyway.

Not until I talk to the toothless lady.

Or we could throw them in the garbage. I don't think she'd notice.

I told you not to touch anything.

Who wants a box full of motel Bibles?

Leave them there.

It seems really stupid to me for someone to save motel Bibles. Maybe they would pass them out. You know, there are people who make a living like that. They check in with the person at the front desk and they ask them for permission to go to the rooms to replace missing Bibles. They replace the missing ones and they steal the towels and the shampoos.

Where do you get that from?

I knew a preacher who would do that. The towels made him enough to supply himself with dope from the boat guys. If you want, I'll look for him and tell him we have some Bibles. We can do business.

Leave them there. They're not yours.

Or maybe we can throw them out, together with all the other things so I can move in.

I said leave them there, maybe they mean something.

I don't think they mean anything. After all, they're Bibles. Do you or do you not have some coke?

Passport

Gustavo Ott

translated by
Heather L. McKay

Left to right: Luis Domingo González, María Brito, and Carolina Torres in the 2003 production of *Passport*, Teatro San Martín de Caracas, directed by Luis Domingo González. Photo by Porfirio Cadillo. Courtesy of Porfirio Cadillo, www.porfiriocadillo.com.

Translator's Note: Moving Borders

To translate Gustavo Ott's *Passport* is to take on the most ironic of tasks: to seek to communicate a work that questions the very possibility of communication, not because language itself is inadequate, but because its reception is always already fatally filtered. Perhaps an optimistic irony is the translator's most comfortable mode, knowing always, as Ortega y Gassett made the liberating observation, that imperfection is the end of any utopian endeavor.

Eugene, a longtime traveler, wakes to find he has arrived at an unknown train station in an unknown country, where the only other people (a soldier and an officer) speak a language he cannot decipher. He hands over his passport, the soldier disappears, and thus begins a dark tragicomedy in the finest Absurdist tradition on the breakdown of human relations. Written in 1987, *Passport* might seem to speak to a pre-European Union Cold War sensibility of well-guarded border crossings, but its theme and emblematic setting are easily transported to today's realities. Startling images of oppression and torture reveal that the unnamed country "far beyond in the distance" could as easily be a Venezuela divided by political misunderstandings or a United States dehumanized by terrorism.

With a play called *Passport*, borders are inevitable. However, when we seek to sketch those borders, we find we are trying to fix a firm outline in constantly shifting sands. We must navigate the obvious frontiers implied by travel, the lines laid down by (military, governmental) authority, personal boundaries, the limits of preconceived ideas, the striations of sedimentary time, the palimpsest of individual identity, and, most of all, the incomprehensible chasm that lies between characters who speak one language but not "the same language," that simply do not, as they repeat again and again, understand each other. With such a web of borders, it seems inevitable that Eugene must be caught up, trapped in a space outlined by its own logic. Our train platform becomes, quite literally, a prison cell.

Just as the audience is always a moving target, the borders of the play itself are also always moving. They shift from moment to moment. They keep the spectator on edge and they also have the power to stir us. Those borders are most clearly drawn and undone by language, and particularly the beauty of a poetic discourse that pierces the play's brutal imagery. And so, as a translator, my first loyalty lay with Ott's poetry, the sounds, rhythms, and repetitions that are his very remedy to catastrophe. To borrow from his *120 Lives a Minute*, "Beauty is not indifferent, it can't be, it never has been." If we are to escape the vertiginous pull of miscommunication, Ott seems to say, we must first find ourselves, not by stepping outside any borders, but by spiraling upward or perhaps inward on a current of poetry. While our play may open and close on the same words in the same scene, the repetition is not fatalistic. Art has the potential to move us, creating both the emotion and the distance necessary for us to make sense of our reality and to take immeasurable journeys without leaving our seats.

Heather L. McKay

Characters

EUGENE – male or female.
OFFICER
SOLDIER

Passport premiered at the Cuarta Pared Theater in Madrid, Spain in October 1991, directed by Javier Yagüe. In 2003 it was produced by Teatro San Martín de Caracas for the Ateneo de Caracas, directed by Luis Domingo González, with the following cast:

EUGENIA	María Brito
OFFICER	David Villegas
SOLDIER	Alfonso Rey

This translation is based on a manuscript provided by the author. The play in Spanish was first published in *8 piezas and two plays*, Vol. I (Caracas: Textoteatro Ediciones and Gobernación del DF, 1991) 203-237. The most recent version of the original text can be found and downloaded at the playwright's website: gustavoott.com.ar.

This is your passport I hold in my hand:
a hemisphere, half red ink, half blue—
as yet untorched by terror, but polluted
perhaps by the gaze of the future. For
example [...] your eyes translated into these
flashing sad idioms. Take this blank page [...]
the last boring national/ tattoos.[...]
Stars shatter on
The epaulets of all the uniforms, the hats
and coats of countries that no longer exist.
I wear your insignia, therefore I wear death's
insignia. Which means that nothing can hurt me.
And with these wings and flames, I pledge
Allegiance to nothing: I can go anywhere.

Carol Muske-Dukes

The action takes place in a train station, in some forgotten country.

1

Train station.

On one side, the Soldier is asleep in a chair that barely holds him up.

On the other, Eugene is asleep in his train seat, a half-open map in his lap. Eugene wakes and the map falls to the floor. A hurrying passenger bumps into him.

We hear the other passengers talking in different languages. Eugene notices a sign in an unknown language that apparently tells the name of the station.

Eugene picks up his suitcase and walks tentatively around the station, listening to the voices reverberating over the loudspeakers, again in an indecipherable language.

Eugene looks for someone to talk to, but no one stops. He sits down on his suitcase. He looks at his watch and can't believe the time.

Then the Soldier wakes up like this is his daily routine and begins to shout.

SOLDIER: Everybody out! Closing time. Everybody out!

(*Eugene sees him and hurries over hopefully.*)

EUGENE: Excuse me, sir, could you, sir, excuse me, I, I...

SOLDIER: Clear the station, we're closing. Come back Monday!

EUGENE: Sir, I have a problem. That is I think I do. I took the wrong...

SOLDIER: Clear the station. Everybody out! We open again on Monday!

EUGENE: I don't understand what you're saying, sir, but...

SOLDIER: Out! Everybody out!

(*The Soldier pays no attention to Eugene, until he turns and looks at him with scorn.*)

EUGENE: Sir, I was going to ask something.

SOLDIER: So. What do you want?

EUGENE: I don't understand your language...

SOLDIER: Huh? What did you say?

EUGENE: What are you saying?

SOLDIER: What the fuck do you want?

EUGENE: Do you know um... Where am I? What country is this?

SOLDIER: I don't understand you. Get an interpreter.

(The Soldier starts to leave but Eugene stops him. The Soldier is annoyed.)

EUGENE: I don't understand. What language do you speak? I don't understand anything, sir...

SOLDIER: Passport.

EUGENE: Excuse me?

SOLDIER: Passport!

EUGENE: Ohh! Passport. I've got it here. Of course, passport.

(Eugene hands him his passport. The Soldier looks through it minutely. He compares the photo to Eugene's face. He checks the stamps.)

SOLDIER: That's strange! It might work.

(The Soldier leaves with the passport. Before going he makes an unintelligible sign to Eugene.)

EUGENE: Wait here, right?

2

Eugene waits a long time. The minutes feel like hours. He slowly is worn down until he slumps onto his suitcase again. There is total silence, broken by the entrance of the Officer, who gestures for him to leave.

OFFICER: Everybody out, leave the platform, you can't stay here.

(Eugene approaches him uncertainly.)

EUGENE: Sir. *(Beat.)* Could you tell me... What city is this?

OFFICER: Clear the platform. Closing time. No more trains till tomorrow.

EUGENE: What did he say? Spain? Tobago?

OFFICER: You have to leave.

EUGENE: I don't understand.

OFFICER: Leave, good-bye. Time to go.

EUGENE: What did you say? Go! Go! For God's sake, where?

OFFICER: *(In defective Spanish.)* You speak Spanish?

EUGENE: Español-Spanish... no, I don't understand Spanish, a little, un poco.

OFFICER: Passport!

EUGENE: I just gave it to the other soldier.

OFFICER: Passport!

EUGENE: I told you...

OFFICER: Don't play games with me.

EUGENE: I gave my passport to the other soldier... he left and he hasn't...

OFFICER: Hmmmmm... no passport. Where are you from?

EUGENE: We're never going to understand each other. I wonder what time it is. *(Looks at his watch.)* It can't be. *(To the Officer.)* Do you have the time? *(Showing him his watch.)* THE-TIME.

OFFICER: A bribe?

EUGENE: Did you say five? What did he say?

OFFICER: He's got no passport. He speaks some gobbledygook and he wants to bribe me.

EUGENE: It's not five. Did you say five thirty? *(Looking at his watch.)* This piece of shit stopped.

OFFICER: Do you have any other identification?

EUGENE: *(Pointing to the watch.)* It doesn't work.

OFFICER: I hate to say this, but you've got a serious problem.

EUGENE: What a ridiculous situation. Christ!

OFFICER: Your doc-u-ments.

EUGENE: I don't understand you, I speak English. I don't understand. I speak En-glish!

OFFICER: *(Trying to imitate.)* Spi.

EUGENE: Spe.

OFFICER: Spi.

EUGENE: E-e-e. Speak.

OFFICER: Spi- Spy? You confess, spy?

EUGENE: I speak English!

OFFICER: *(Takes out handcuffs and puts them on Eugene. Eugene screams, but we don't hear him.)* You're a damn...

3

Music.

The Officer takes Eugene to his desk and shoves him into a chair. Beside him, his suitcase. The Soldier appears behind Eugene, who at first doesn't see him.

OFFICER: ... Spy!

SOLDIER: He confessed?

OFFICER: And he's got no passport.

EUGENE: I don't understand you. I don't understand anything at all. What are you saying?

OFFICER: Passport!

(Eugene looks to the heavens with a desperate gesture.)

OFFICER: Where did you come from? The North, the South?

SOLDIER: There's something strange about you.

OFFICER: You must be from the South.

SOLDIER: Open a file on him and we'll throw him in the hole.

OFFICER: I'm going to explain the situation to you. You know what you've done is illegal?

EUGENE: Pardon? *(Desperately.)* I don't understand. I don't understand anything.

SOLDIER: He says he doesn't understand.

OFFICER: You speak his language?

SOLDIER: Some.

OFFICER: How come you speak so many languages?

SOLDIER: I watch a lot of TV.

OFFICER: Tell him he has to sign this paper.

SOLDIER: *(To Eugene, who can't see him yet.)* Sign the paper, you worm.

EUGENE: I don't understand what you're saying.

SOLDIER: *(To Officer.)* He says he understands perfectly.

OFFICER: Excellent... *(Writing.)* "... I understand that I am in a terrible illegal situation and I voluntarily renounce all my inalienable rights..."

SOLDIER: Yes, that's it.

EUGENE: *(Trying to see the Soldier.)* Yes?

SOLDIER: You just say yes, that's all.

EUGENE: Yes?

OFFICER: Because if you've entered the country without a passport, there are severe penalties.

EUGENE: I don't understand.

SOLDIER: He says he's aware of that.

OFFICER: Good. So: did you come alone or with others?

EUGENE: I don't understand...

OFFICER: *(To Eugene.)* Did you come from the South?

EUGENE: I don't understand.

OFFICER: What did he say?

SOLDIER: He comes from the South, from a city up in the mountains, with a seaport. He has a wife, a lover, and a son he hasn't seen for a long time, but that doesn't bother him as much as knowing that he doesn't care.

EUGENE: Sir, could you please... could you please explain what is going on?

OFFICER: Passport!

EUGENE: But I just told you I gave it to a... *(Finally seeing the Soldier.)* To him! I gave my passport to him!

SOLDIER: He says he's got no passport and he doesn't care because he thinks you're an asshole and that I'm very intelligent, but handsome.

OFFICER: He said that?

SOLDIER: Actually he used the word gorgeous, more than handsome.

EUGENE: I guess you told him you have my passport.

OFFICER: What was he doing when you found him?

SOLDIER: Looking all around and I think he was trying to plant plastic explosives in baby strollers. Isn't that right?

EUGENE: Yes, that's it... *(To the Officer.)* You see. All cleared up. The Soldier here has my passport and he already looked it over. Right?

OFFICER: What he said. Is it true?

EUGENE: Yes, he has it.

OFFICER: For the last time: Passport!

EUGENE: Jesus, I gave my passport to...

OFFICER: Passport!

EUGENE: Fuck this!

OFFICER: Passport!

EUGENE: Assholes!

OFFICER: This suspect is suspicious. Maybe he does understand us and he's just playing dumb.

SOLDIER: Or he's calling us names. Insulting us...

OFFICER: But you understand what he says.

SOLDIER: When he talks fast I don't understand much.

EUGENE: I want to talk with the consulate.

OFFICER: Passport!

EUGENE: I already told you I gave it to him...

> (*Eugene tries to touch the Soldier.*
>
> *The Soldier hits him with the rifle butt. Eugene blacks out.*
>
> *The Soldier and Officer look at each other conspiratorially.*)

OFFICER: Let him sleep a while. Go check his luggage.

> (*The Soldier goes through the suitcase. He takes everything out, piece by piece.*)

OFFICER: Check it carefully. We don't want a replay of my brother and the bomb.

SOLDIER: That's all foreigners know how to do... plant bombs.

OFFICER: A bomb killed my brother.

SOLDIER: Oh. Yeah? In an attack?

OFFICER: No, it went off when he was playing with it.

SOLDIER: He was playing with a bomb?

OFFICER: He wasn't too bright.

SOLDIER: I guess not. Runs in the family, huh?

OFFICER: Don't get smart with me or I'll put you back on toilet duty.

SOLDIER: Sorry, sir. It won't happen again.

OFFICER: No one in your family's died?

SOLDIER: What do you mean?

OFFICER: With the bombs and all that crap...

SOLDIER: My dad.

OFFICER: Ah...

SOLDIER: A foreigner. She was crossing the border with her hand luggage. She dropped it. My father tried to be polite and booommm!

(Eugene comes to, but remains on the floor.)

EUGENE: What happened? Why'd you hit me?

SOLDIER: He's awake.

OFFICER: We better frisk him. He could be armed.

EUGENE: Why'd you hit me? What did I do?

SOLDIER: I hit you hard so you could take a little nap.

OFFICER: *(To Eugene.)* The captain warned me there are lots of terrorists... You need to understand, we've had many attacks.

EUGENE: I guess that's an apology.

OFFICER: Why only yesterday a commercial flight...

EUGENE: Thank you... thank you, we're all nervous, I understand.

OFFICER: *(Helps Eugene to his feet.)* You've come to a country that has many enemies.

EUGENE: It's okay. The pain's going away.

OFFICER: *(Taking Eugene by the arm.)* And that's why I need to know where your passport is.

EUGENE: Yes?

SOLDIER: Look, let's get this over with fast. We need to know who you are, where you're from, and what you're planning...

EUGENE: I think they understand me now.

OFFICER: It would be better if you didn't speak while I'm...

EUGENE: Fine. It's all forgotten. Could you tell me how I can get to...?

OFFICER: Passport!

EUGENE: They'll never understand me!

SOLDIER: *(Checking the suitcase.)* There's some books here.

OFFICER: Books? In what language?

SOLDIER: I don't know. Greek, Chinese, Peruvian.

OFFICER: Greek Peruvian? Are you Greek Peruvian?

EUGENE: Look, I don't know what you're saying. I was on the train and I must've missed a transfer. I've got a ticket to... my ticket!

(Eugene starts to rifle through his jacket pockets, but his movements seem very dangerous. The Soldier, terrified, points his gun at him and shouts. The Officer also pulls out his revolver and aims it at Eugene.)

BOTH: What is this?! What are you doing? Show your hands. Show your hands or we'll shoot, you filthy pig. On the ground, now, get down, show your hands. Show your hands!!!

(The Soldier grabs Eugene while the Officer keeps his gun on him. They shove him to the wall. They frisk him again.)

SOLDIER: *(Checking his pockets.)* I think I found his wallet.

OFFICER: Check it carefully...

SOLDIER: Hey, look!

OFFICER: What's that?

SOLDIER: Money. Foreign currency.

OFFICER: *(Hits Eugene.)* Did you declare this money at the border?

EUGENE: That's mine.

SOLDIER: Here's more money. And cigarettes.

OFFICER: *(Hits Eugene.)* Cigarettes? Drugs?

EUGENE: You're breaking my bones!

OFFICER: So, attempting to smuggle in contraband.

EUGENE: Now what?

OFFICER: Foreign currency, huh? You know this money's illegal in this country?

SOLDIER: No passport and trying to destroy our economy and our children with foreign currency and drugs.

EUGENE: What did I say? What did I do?

OFFICER: What are you? A smuggler from the South?

EUGENE: Let me explain.

OFFICER: We know what to do with people like you, you terrorist, you fucking smuggler.

EUGENE: Somebody help me!

(The last blow knocks Eugene to his knees. They turn him over. Tense music.)

OFFICER: You have something to declare?

EUGENE: I don't understand you!

OFFICER: Where's your passport?

EUGENE: What?

OFFICER: Passport!

(They blindfold him.)

EUGENE: What's going on? I didn't do anything!

SOLDIER: Don't say anything that can be used against you.

OFFICER: Don't waste your time, he doesn't understand a word.

EUGENE: I didn't do anything. Don't you understand? I want to talk to... I want to talk to someone who understands me.

OFFICER: Shut him up and turn off the lights.

SOLDIER: *(Preparing his hands.)* Yes, sir.

(The Officer exits. The Soldier and Eugene are left alone. The Soldier cracks his knuckles. Music.)

4

Eugene, blindfolded. The Soldier is asleep beside him, snoring. Behind them, the Officer eats soup, slurping noisily.

EUGENE: I've never had any problems with the police or the military. I've never broken any laws. Actually, I've never even been inside a jail. I've never even seen one in my whole life.

Can you take this blindfold off?

I swear I won't see anything.

Nothing like this ever happened to me before.

I thought things like this didn't really happen.

Maybe to other people. But not me. I suppose my government has already requested my release. They're probably talking about me on the news. There was a time when I thought I should have terrible things happen to me so I could have experiences and grow. To have incredible things happen to me while I was still young. Fantastic stories to tell. But nothing ever happened to me. I guess this whole situation will be one of my experiences.

What I don't know is what it's good for.

I guess it must mean something.

What do you think it means, huh?

Huh?

What do you think it all means?

OFFICER: I don't understand what you're saying. You could be insulting me in that weird language and here I am, thinking you're saying your prayers. Shut up!

EUGENE: So you're thinking what I'm thinking. That this whole experience will turn out fine. And I'll get a lot out of it... I'm glad...

I'm glad you think so.

OFFICER: Maybe you're speaking in code. Communicating with your accomplices. Via... via antenna... or some way we don't know. Through the air. That's it. You're communicating through the air...

(The Soldier wakes up.)

SOLDIER: What happened?

OFFICER: You were snoring.

SOLDIER: I don't snore. I was dreaming, dreaming I was someone else. *(To Eugene.)* Do you dream you're someone else?

EUGENE: *(To the Soldier.)* I think I know you. Yes... yes... yes...

SOLDIER: *(Imitating him.)* Yes... yes... yes...

EUGENE: Your voice sounds familiar. Even if I can't see you, I can feel you. Your voice. Your voice sounds like that soldier I saw a few days ago at the train station. The one who took my passport.

SOLDIER: Passport?

EUGENE: Exactly. Could you take this blindfold off...?

SOLDIER: *(Making fun of him.)* Yes... yes... yes...

EUGENE: Yes? Yes?

SOLDIER: Yes... yes... yes... *(Laughs.)* You're a fraud. Your passport isn't worth the paper it's printed on.

EUGENE: What's that?

SOLDIER: Yes... yes... yes...

EUGENE: I remember the face of the man who took my passport. Because when I first saw him, he reminded me of someone.

Someone I saw... on TV back home. It was a report on how young people were training to defend our country against some enemy. In a little room, maybe like this one. They were packed in, must have been at least eighty of them...

No clothes. No room. Fighting for breath.

And you were asking them: Do you want to defend your country?

Do you want to die for your country?

And they said yes.

They'd give everything for their country. You talk like that soldier.

But I guess soldiers sound the same everywhere.

(The Soldier takes the blindfold from Eugene's eyes.)

EUGENE: Thank you! Finally! You!!

(The Soldier uses the cloth to gag Eugene, who can no longer speak.)

SOLDIER: Let's hear how you say your prayers now.

(The Soldier takes a picture of himself with his prisoner, as though he were a trophy. Then he takes him to a chair at center stage.)

5

The Officer goes over to Eugene, gets him out of the chair and removes the handcuffs. Eugene tries to remove his gag, but the Officer warns him not to. He takes Eugene to a shower.

OFFICER: We're waiting for a call from headquarters to see what we're going to do with you. But these things take time, while they look for the Commander, then he looks over your documents, the reports, the files. The commander will call when your country contacts him or you are deported or charged and sentenced under our laws. In the meantime, you can get cleaned up. Understand?

(Eugene nods, automatically.)

"Luna Llena" by Simón Díaz plays, duet version with Ilán Chester.

They remove Eugene's clothes, but not his gag. He stands in underwear or naked and they throw water on him. Eugene screams. Then they dunk his head in a bucket of water.

What looks like a hair washing at the moment reminds us of torture. They dunk his head up to three times in a bucket of water.

After a pause, the Officer puts a belt around Eugene's neck, pushes him down on four legs, like a dog, and the Soldier takes his picture while the Officer gives a "thumbs up." It's the kind of picture a tourist would take.

Then, they put a pointed black hood on his head.

They attach cables to him that aren't connected to anything, but which he thinks are. They stand him up on a chair, make him open his arms wide. The Soldier and Officer scare him, pretending they will electrocute him.

They laugh. Eugene catches on and sits down in the chair, humiliated.

The Officer takes off the hood. Eugene brings to mind Munch's The Scream. The Officer hands him a towel. Eugene dries off. Shivers with cold.

The two look at each other.

Suddenly, very nicely, the Officer takes the gag from his mouth.)

OFFICER: *(Politely.)* I hope they haven't hurt you.

6

Then the Soldier enters. He carries a tray with a glass and a jar of water. The Officer sits down in a chair and orders the Soldier to give Eugene water. Eugene takes it.

EUGENE: I don't understand you, you see?

OFFICER: I know we don't speak the same language, but...

EUGENE: I don't understand you, sir, not a word...

OFFICER: But we understand each other... don't we?

Would you like a little of this precious liquid?

EUGENE: *(To please him.)* Thank you...

OFFICER: Yes?

EUGENE: Yes...

(The Officer orders the Soldier to serve him water. Eugene drinks.)

EUGENE: Thank you... thank you... I knew there must have been some misunderstanding...

OFFICER: Are you still thirsty?

EUGENE: What?

OFFICER: Thirsty?

EUGENE: I-do-not-speak-your-lan-guage.

OFFICER: You know. Drink... to drink.

(Makes drinking motion.)

EUGENE: Oh! To drink... Yes, yes... yes...

OFFICER: More water, quickly...!

(The Soldier serves Eugene more water. Eugene drinks it, but leaves a little. The Soldier dumps it out.)

OFFICER: Now. It so happens I'm a government worker at this train station. I live in this very town. I'm from here, but you see I'm a man of the world, a humanist.

EUGENE: Thank you very much. That's very kind of you...

OFFICER: Even though I don't speak your language, I know exactly what you're going through.

EUGENE: I guess you spoke with the consulate by now...

OFFICER: *(Makes drinking motion.)* Do you want more water?

EUGENE: No, thank you.

OFFICER: Fine. Give him more water.

(The Soldier gives him more water. Eugene accepts it with a sigh.)

OFFICER: You have a nice face. You don't look like a terrorist or a smuggler. Do you want more water? *(Makes drinking motion.)*

EUGENE: No, thank you.

OFFICER: Fine. Give him more water.

(The Soldier gives him water. Eugene drinks it with difficulty.)

OFFICER: You have a nice face...

EUGENE: *(Standing.)* Did you say we're leaving now?

OFFICER: No, you're no criminal...

EUGENE: *(Sitting back down.)* We're staying.

OFFICER: But you must cooperate... Do you want more water? *(Makes drinking motion.)*

EUGENE: No, thank you, really. Not anymore. It's enough. I don't want any. No.

OFFICER: Fine. Give him more water.

(The Soldier gives him water. Eugene drinks it but spills most down his front.)

OFFICER: We live far beyond in the distance. Foreigners almost never come here. People from our own country don't even come here. People from neighboring regions don't come here, so you have to understand, a person like you, who... Do you want more water? *(Makes drinking motion.)*

EUGENE: No, please! I'm begging you! Please! No more!

OFFICER: Fine. Give him more water.

(The Soldier gives him water. Eugene feels like he is going to explode.)

OFFICER: Because we have plenty of water here, you know? There are lots of rivers and open sewers.

EUGENE: I wish I could understand you!

OFFICER: Now!

(At the Officer's order, the Soldier takes an old microphone from the tray and shoves it in Eugene's face.)

SOLDIER: Repeat that.

EUGENE: What?

OFFICER: Repeat what you said.

EUGENE: What?

OFFICER: "Ungerstanyu."

EUGENE: Understand you.

SOLDIER: "Untersandoo."

EUGENE: Understand you!

OFFICER: I certainly hope you haven't said anything that could be used against you.

EUGENE: They probably want to figure out what language I speak. Get a translator...

OFFICER: Okay, that's the way, my friend. Now repeat after me: "I gould unersand hoo."

EUGENE: Understand you...

SOLDIER: Understand you...

EUGENE: Understand you...

(All laugh.)

OFFICER: Excellent.

EUGENE: You liked that. Understand you, understand you. *(Laughs.)* You're starting to understand me a little...

OFFICER: Excellent, now say this word with me: *(After a pause.)* Pass...

EUGENE: Pass.

OFFICER: Port... Passport.

EUGENE: Oh my God!

OFFICER and SOLDIER: Passport!

EUGENE: You haven't understood a word I've said.

OFFICER: Say Passport!

EUGENE: What kind of hell is this!?!

(The Officer loses his temper and grabs Eugene violently.)

OFFICER: You have to have some kind of identification! Everyone does! No one is special here!

OFFICER and SOLDIER: Passport! Passport. Passport!

EUGENE: Good Lord, what is this place!?

(Music. "El loco Juan Carabina" by Simón Díaz. Officer and Soldier drag Eugene to one side of the stage.)

7

Eugene dresses.

The stage changes colors, as though time were passing outside a window.

We hear people in the distance.

Eugene gets up, goes to the window.

He looks out.

He sees the Soldier, at the mirror, fixing himself up the best he can. He puts on cologne and doesn't like the smell.

To the other side, the Officer, dressed as an ice cream vendor, pushes his cart slowly.

Lights up on a park.

The Soldier heads that way, with a newspaper and a flower, and waits...

Voices, especially of children.

The Soldier tries to swat a fly and looks at Eugene.

Eugene waves to him, but the Soldier ignores him.

The Ice Cream Man/Officer takes out an ice cream and eats it, staring at the ground.

The Soldier loses his patience. He crumples up the paper and steps on the flower.

Then he regrets it, picks up the flower, now in bad shape, and puts it in his pocket.

The Ice Cream Man/Officer pushes his cart as though moving into a strong wind.

The Soldier returns to the mirror, musses his hair furiously.

The Ice Cream Man/Officer walks ahead of his cart now as though he were fleeing from it, but the cart follows him, like a monster.

8

The Soldier goes over to Eugene.

SOLDIER: Hey, foreigner. What are the women like in your country?

EUGENE: What's that?

SOLDIER: I said what are the women like in your country?

EUGENE: Oh! Why did I come here?

SOLDIER: Right, the women. So? Are they... um... wild or submissive?

EUGENE: I guess I made a mistake.

SOLDIER: I like them submissive.

EUGENE: I was looking for a long-distance train, but I fell asleep and they switched tracks. No one woke me up. No one said anything.

SOLDIER: You're lucky. Not here. Here they're butch. Strong. With mustaches. Not like the women you see on TV.

EUGENE: Exactly. Days went by and I got used to traveling. The mountains, the bridges. The foreign countries. Everything I'd never seen before.

SOLDIER: They make them exercise and they get these disgusting muscles. I like my women soft and delicate.

EUGENE: You say you like bridges too?

SOLDIER: I love them.

EUGENE: Me too.

SOLDIER: In your country are the women loving or do they ask for money?

EUGENE: That's it, just like you say. Days and bridges went by. I lost my maps. My bearings. The world's a big place. And everywhere there are stations, people saying good-bye. Train tracks, roads, switchmen, bells...

SOLDIER: ... Yeah, I know what you mean, even if I don't understand a word you're saying. We all feel the same way about women. Whether it's in Chinese or Croatian. I've been divorced three times. And all three times I hated them more than I ever loved them. You married? A widower? I'd love to be a widower.

EUGENE: All right. I'll explain the best I can.

I traveled for too many reasons. Maybe it was travel instead of picking up a gun.

Because... because I believed in all those mistaken theories about time and distance...

Because of a broken dream.

Because I believed in heroic deeds. Because I was brave, and stupid, and foolish.

Because I was in love with life, even though I was dead.

Because I wanted to praise a world that can't even stand itself. Because the streets smelled of the scent of couples who swore eternal love and could never stay together.

Because in my country nothing grew anymore, not even weeds.

Because there they stole the roots, the trees, the winds. Because there were schools for the blind and deaf to educate specialists, counselors, and artists. Because... because *(Laughs.)* I think I left my country because there were so many gray vases.

Maybe I took that train to go through the insanity of this very moment!

(Furious, loud.) I took it because I felt like it and I didn't know what I was doing!

I took it because right now I'm sweating right down to my balls!

SOLDIER: Don't get so worked up. She's not worth it. Even if she is that amazing woman who makes you feel all that. She's not worth it. Think about yourself. No one else matters. Okay? Okay.

EUGENE: Okay?

SOLDIER: Okay!

EUGENE: Understand you...

SOLDIER: Understand you...

(They both laugh. The Officer takes off the ice cream vendor's uniform.)

SOLDIER: *(Laughs.)* You see? Now we're understanding each other.

EUGENE: I don't know how, but you understood everything.

(The Officer approaches them with a plate and some bread.)

OFFICER: Telling secrets?

SOLDIER: He's as broken as everyone else

OFFICER: What, did you think people were better in other places?

SOLDIER: It makes me feel better to know they're just as fucked up.

OFFICER: Me too. *(Shows Eugene the food.)* You hungry?

EUGENE: *(Pleased.)* It's about time, I was hungry.

OFFICER: What? You're not hungry?

EUGENE: I'm dying for something to eat.

OFFICER: Not hungry, ah? Don't you trust the food?

Soldier: Don't worry. We're not going to poison you. If we wanted to kill you, you'd be swimming underground by now.

(*The Officer breaks the bread in two and gives the smaller half to the Soldier.*)

Officer: You'll get hungry soon enough. Then you'll have to talk to ask for food.

(*The two men eat.*)

Soldier: Leave him alone. So maybe he plants bombs, but he's not a bad guy.

(*Eugene reaches out to ask for a bit of bread from the Soldier. The Soldier is moved and goes to him. He gives the crumbs to Eugene, who accepts them happily. He eats the crumbs like a happy mouse. Music.*)

9

Eugene lies down and sleeps. The Officer fills out forms while the Soldier, sitting in his chair, tries to whistle. He can't. He hums a ballad until he realizes that he doesn't know it very well. He starts over again and makes another mistake.

Officer: You're losing your ear.

(*Now the Officer hums the whole stanza.*)

Officer: That's how it goes.

(*The Soldier tries again, but once again goes out of tune. The Officer laughs.*)

Soldier: I'd like to know where the tracks end.

Officer: The tracks never end. They come to one station, like this one, and then keep going to another and then another.

Soldier: You've traveled. You've seen the world.

Officer: It's hard to remember it.

Soldier: If I traveled, I'd never forget my way.

Officer: If you traveled, you'd forget even your own self. Why don't you tell me the story about your father and the bomb again?

Soldier: It was at the border and she was a foreigner. A beautiful blonde dressed in blue, who spoke like an angel...

(The Officer and Soldier's voices fade. Little by little we stop hearing the Soldier's voice, although he still gestures as though speaking animatedly. Eugene stands and stares at the Soldier telling his story, but neither the Officer nor the Soldier realize that Eugene is awake.)

EUGENE: ... I think that blow must have affected my hearing... I can't hear anything. I've gone deaf. Or everyone got quiet so I wouldn't hear them. Or they're pretending they're talking to trick me.

(A distant beating is heard.)

But I hear something.

I hear...

What is that? It's... it's... it's...

A heart. It's my heart. I've never heard it beat so hard. It's loud. Like it's trying to tell me something.

(The beating grows still louder.)

It's close, like a lament. It's making me nervous. I hear you already, that's enough, that's enough, enough!

(The beating stops. The sound of flowing water.)

Now what? Water. Currents moving inside of me. I think it's... It's my blood, I can hear it moving in my veins. I can hear it like a raging river.

(Strange noises.)

And now? The sound of my thoughts. As they forge a path. As they rise up. As they try to be me.

I can hear the sound of my organs.

The beat of my eyelashes across my eyes,

the scrape of my lips parting.

The roar of my saliva as it falls through my insides and breaks against my stomach.

The howl of the wind entering and leaving my lungs.

I can hear everything going on inside my body and nothing else.

I think I've gone stone deaf.

(At the end of Eugene's words we once again hear the Soldier whistling a ballad.)

SOLDIER: Tomorrow I'm leaving for the South.

OFFICER: The South? What for?

SOLDIER: They have things there.

OFFICER: The only thing in the South is people.

SOLDIER: I don't care, I'm leaving for the South.

OFFICER: They have worse passports there. And dangerous crimes.

SOLDIER: In the South they've got information. You know what's going on. Here, for all we know we could be... we could be defending a border that doesn't even exist anymore and we'd find out when it was already too late. Or maybe they changed the laws and we don't know about it. Maybe they don't need soldiers anymore and everyone's sitting at home watching TV. Everyone but me.

Maybe there's a new boss and we're still taking orders from the old ones.

Maybe there are guys like him, who speak other languages and read strange books, and know what they're talking about.

OFFICER: You think this guy knows what he's talking about?

SOLDIER: Absolutely.

OFFICER: How do you know?

SOLDIER: Because he looks sure of himself. He looks you in the eye. He's a man of conviction.

OFFICER: I've seen bomb-makers that had that same look like wedding cake dolls.

(Their voices fade away again, although they continue their animated conversation. We only hear Eugene, who watches them.)

EUGENE: There's like a murmuring. Something far off. I wonder what they're saying? Gov... government stuff, I'm sure. National concerns. *(He listens.)*

I bet they're talking about me. And my stupid mistake. They look like good people. Honest. Intelligent. Too bad they can't understand me! I bet we'd be good friends.

Even if they are so close and I can't hear them and they can't hear me either.

(Sea sounds. Eugene, surprised.)

But I...

I hear.

I hear waves, like a sea inside me.

I hear the sea, like it's lapping at me, covering my body.

And I can hear what's on the other side of this wall.

I hear a soldier's girlfriend who comes and doesn't find what she was promised.

I hear an ice cream vendor who's eaten nothing but his own merchandise for weeks.

I hear a boy in a park, who they make cry so they can take his picture.

I hear a train pulling in and now it's gone, long gone.

I hear different voices, in other languages and mine.

I can hear the noise of five foreign cities.

I hear the whistle of traffic cops in Hong Kong. A plane touching down in Frankfurt, even the sobs of a forgotten bride in Vancouver.

(Eugene, deaf, impassioned.)

I hear music and footsteps.

A party thousands of miles away. The tinkling of laughter and raised glasses. Best wishes in five languages I don't speak, but can understand.

I hear the scratch of a blind man trying to read Braille.

I hear bad news in Morse code.

I can hear long-distance declarations of love and two strangers meeting in a train station like a picture postcard.

I hear the applause of an appreciative audience in some unknown theater of the world. I hear the scraping of the clouds across the moon and New Year's fireworks.

(Suddenly, Eugene is nervous.)

I hear a gunshot. Someone falling. Someone running away. A door slamming and a radio sputtering out tomorrow's news like it was already five days old.

I hear a crowd moving toward the same place and I can hear that they don't know why.

I can hear so far away, but them, they're right next to me, and I can hardly hear them... Could it be that I'm not here? Or that I'm dying? Or am I already dead?

10

Suddenly, the Soldier and Officer are pressing in on Eugene.

OFFICER: What is he saying?

SOLDIER: I think he's praying.

OFFICER: That was scary.

SOLDIER: Like he was possessed

OFFICER: You think it's the devil?

SOLDIER: Or a fever?

OFFICER: Or he's crazy?

SOLDIER: Or he was singing. *(To Eugene.)* Were you singing? What was all that you were saying?

OFFICER: Who were you insulting? What bad words were you using?

SOLDIER: Talk, prisoner. Talk...

EUGENE: *(Terrified.)* Yes... yes... yes...

OFFICER: What is all this "yes... yes... yes."

SOLDIER: He repeats it constantly.

OFFICER: What do you think it means?

SOLDIER: It's like some kind of greeting. Like "hello."

OFFICER: Or maybe it's an affirmation. Maybe "yes" means "yes."

SOLDIER: I don't think so, "yes" doesn't sound anything like "yes."

OFFICER: But maybe in another language, "yes" it does.

SOLDIER: "Yes?"

OFFICER: "Yes."

SOLDIER: They're not the same. Watch. *(To Eugene.)* Look, foreigner, you want a bullet between the eyes?

EUGENE: Yes... yes... yes... *(They laugh.)*

SOLDIER and OFFICER: Yes... yes... yes... *(They laugh.)*

SOLDIER: You want me to cut off your toes and serve them to you for lunch?

EUGENE: Yes... yes... yes...

SOLDIER and OFFICER: Yes... yes... yes... *(They laugh.)*

SOLDIER: Now say: "I am a beast of burden."

(The Soldier gestures for Eugene to repeat what he has just said.)

SOLDIER: Now say: "I am a beast of burden."

EUGENE: I am a beast of burden.

SOLDIER and OFFICER: Yes... yes... yes... *(They laugh.)*

OFFICER: My turn. Let me. *(To Eugene.)* Say: "I am an animal. I am a filthy animal."

EUGENE: *(Accusingly.)* Filthy animal.

OFFICER: What?

EUGENE: Filthy animal.

SOLDIER: I think he called you...

OFFICER: I'm a filthy animal?

EUGENE: Yes... yes... yes...

OFFICER: Son of a bitch! After all I've done for you, this is how you repay me. I'll kill you.

SOLDIER: Relax, boss. He can't understand you. He doesn't know what he's saying.

OFFICER: He called me a "filthy animal."

SOLDIER: He was repeating, like a parrot. Like a little wild animal. Right?

OFFICER: Sometimes I think he's just playing dumb.

SOLDIER: He doesn't understand us. For example, watch this. *(To Eugene.)* Are you afraid?

(Silence.)

SOLDIER: Are you afraid?

EUGENE: Yes.

SOLDIER: Do you like being afraid?

EUGENE: Afraid.

SOLDIER: Do you like it?

(Eugene gestures that he doesn't understand.)

SOLDIER: See? He doesn't understand a thing.

(The Soldier goes back to whistling his ballad, a bit more in key now. He goes back to his chair.)

OFFICER: Why don't you tell me that story again, about your father and the bomb?

SOLDIER: It was at the border and she was a brunette in a red suit...

(The telephone rings. This is the most surprising sound in the world to the Soldier and Officer. They are startled, then turn to look at each other in terror.)

SOLDIER: I thought it was disconnected.

OFFICER: It's never rung before.

SOLDIER: Well, you'd better answer it, sir.

OFFICER: You do it.

SOLDIER: No, I can't.

OFFICER: Are you afraid?

SOLDIER: You're the commanding officer at this post. It's your duty.

OFFICER: But you could pretend to be my secretary or something like that.

SOLDIER: I'm a soldier, not a secretary.

OFFICER: Go on. You answer. I can put you on toilet duty again.

SOLDIER: Well, since you asked so nicely.

(The Soldier answers the telephone. Looks serious.)

SOLDIER: Hello? Yes, sir... Yes, sir!... Yes, sir?... "Yes, sir"... <u>Yes, sir</u>... **Yes, sir**... Of course, sir... Right away, sir.

One moment. *(To the Officer.)* It's for you.

OFFICER: Who is it?

SOLDIER: A superior.

OFFICER: *(Terrified, answers.)* Yes sir... yes, it's me... Yes...

The prisoner arrived five days ago... Yes... yes... He's eaten well and he's been chattering away... He's had one bath, but he doesn't smell bad. We've had one bath too and the Soldier you can already tell... Yes... Yes...

(Suddenly he frowns and looks at Eugene. Eugene is frightened.)

Are you sure?

Orders? Did we look in his wallet?

(The Soldier picks up Eugene and takes his wallet. He hands it to the Officer, who looks through it as he talks.)

We already did that and of course... of course... yes... yes...

(Pulls a piece of paper from Eugene's wallet.)

Here it is. Yes sir, just like you said. Excellent idea. At your service. Don't worry. But, before we hang up, clarify one thing for me, so we can proceed.

Yes, tell me:

What's the weather like there?

What do the women wear?

How much does a beer cost?

What's the President's name?

(Waits for answers.)

Hello? Hello? Hello?

(Hangs up. Eugene looks at him, hopefully.)

EUGENE: Is everything all right? Is it all worked out? You realized the mistake now?

(Theme music. The Soldier and the Officer look at each other and go over to Eugene. They take him by the arms and move him to center stage, very violently.)

EUGENE: But... but... but... For God's sake, don't make a mistake. I hope not. Don't do anything to me...

SOLDIER: You'd better be quiet...

EUGENE: Wait... wait...

OFFICER: Move!

EUGENE: What did he say? What's going on?

OFFICER: We've found something important. We received information from the capital. They gave us information and we corroborated it with your ID.

(The Officer hands the Soldier the piece of paper.)

SOLDIER: What's this supposed to be?

OFFICER: It was in his wallet. It's falling apart.

SOLDIER: Yes, but what is it?

OFFICER: An ID.

SOLDIER: Do you understand what it says?

OFFICER: Perfectly.

SOLDIER: But... what language is it in?

OFFICER: Ours.

SOLDIER: Ours?

OFFICER: *(Reads.)* "Driver's License. Eugene Gant, Address, city, etc. etc. Date: July 19th." It's got his picture. Like a snapshot.

SOLDIER: *(To Eugene.)* Is this yours?

(Eugene looks at it. He hardly recognizes it.)

OFFICER: Is this you?

(Eugene stares at it.)

SOLDIER: It's you!!!

(Eugene trembles.)

OFFICER: Why are you pretending you don't understand us? Why are you pretending you speak some other language? You're from here. This is your country. You speak our language. We know exactly who you are.

They called from the capital with your information. You work in the Ministry of Agriculture. You receive applications. You stamp them. You process them. You file them. Why are you pretending to be someone else?

(They hand the ID to Eugene, who looks at it happily. He begins straightening himself up.)

SOLDIER: What are you hiding? Why are you pretending to be a foreigner? Don't you love your country? Don't you remember it at all?

OFFICER: After all this country's done for you! *(Enraged.)* Do you recognize this paper? Doesn't all this look familiar?

EUGENE: Yes... it's.

It's me. I was twenty and I thought I'd never die. The whole world was a cake and I was the birthday boy. It's my driver's license. And that's my name.

My name is Eugene. Eugene Gant... and... Oh my God! I'm in my own country. This is where I'm from!

But everything's changed so much!

OFFICER: What is he saying?

SOLDIER: He's very sick. He's traveled across 12 continents and in all of them the soldiers were happy, except here. He doesn't like it here. He wants to go to the South.

OFFICER: Fine. The best thing to do is get rid of him.

(The two men begin to dress Eugene as in Scene One and return his suitcase to him.)

EUGENE: I'm back and I don't recognize a thing. They all talk so different, so strange, so foreign.

OFFICER: Get him out of here.

(The Officer begins to exit, but first he pulls the telephone from the wall and takes it with him.)

OFFICER: *(Almost crying.)* I'm sick of the capital!

(The Officer exits.)

SOLDIER: *(To Eugene.)* All right, off you go.

EUGENE: To where?

SOLDIER: To where the tracks end.

EUGENE: But I live in this country, on the way to somewhere, very close to someplace.

SOLDIER: You'll go on stumbling around the world.

EUGENE: We're talking now, we understand each other

SOLDIER: Yes, now we understand you. *(Returns Eugene's passport.)* But we don't care.

(The Soldier takes hold of Eugene to throw him out.)

EUGENE: Thank you.

SOLDIER: Good-bye.

> (*Throws Eugene out. Sound of trains, cars, planes, a whirlwind. Eugene meets the noise head on. We hear the same music that opened the play.*
>
> *The Soldier goes to his chair. He hums the tune and falls asleep.*
>
> *Eugene picks up the map, straightens, shakes his head. We hear the other passengers and people talking in different languages. Eugene notices a sign in an unknown language that, apparently, shows the station name.*
>
> *Eugene picks up his suitcase and walks tentatively around the station, listening to the voices reverberating over the loudspeakers, again in an indecipherable language.*
>
> *Eugene looks for someone to talk to, but no one stops. He sits down on his suitcase. He looks at his watch and can't believe the time.*
>
> *No one is nearby, only voices.*
>
> *Then the Soldier wakes up like this is his daily routine and begins to shout. It's the same scene that began the play, only this time, the dialogue is covered by the music, at top volume, and we see the scene in shadows.*)

SOLDIER: Everybody out! Closing time. Everybody out!

> (*Eugene sees him and hurries over hopefully.*)

EUGENE: Excuse me, sir, could you, sir, excuse me, I, I...

SOLDIER: Clear the station, we're closing. Come back Monday!

EUGENE: I don't understand what you're saying, sir, but...

SOLDIER: Out! Everybody out!

EUGENE: I don't understand your language...

SOLDIER: Huh? What did you say?

EUGENE: What are you saying?

SOLDIER: What the fuck do you want?

EUGENE: Do you know um... Where am I? What country is this?

SOLDIER: I don't understand you. Passport!

EUGENE: Ohh! Passport. I've got it here. Of course, passport. I must have it here somewhere.

(*Eugene takes out his passport and hands it to the Soldier.*

Black.)

Heather L. McKay (M.F.A. Translation – University of Iowa) is Translator for the Teatro San Martín de Caracas, as well as the Founder and General Coordinator of *In Translation* (intranslation.com.ar), a website dedicated to promoting English translations of Spanish-language plays.

McKay has translated several plays and screenplays, as well as short stories and poetry, by Spanish and Latin American writers, including: Lope de Vega, Rómulo Gallegos, Nestor Caballero, Gustavo Ott, Santiago García, Ernesto Caballero, Berta Iriarte, Domingo Palma, Patricia Suárez, and Marcelo Rodríguez.

For her translations McKay has received an honorable mention in the McLaren Memorial Comedy Playwriting Competition (*Minor Leagues*), the Lawrence S. Epstein Playwriting Award (*Who Ever Said I Was a Good Girl?*), and the Princess Grace (finalist - *80 Teeth, 4 Feet, and 500 Pounds*). Her translations have also been published in anthologies by Meriwether Publishing, used in bilingual productions by GALA Hispanic Theatre (Washington, DC) and Repertorio Español (New York), and produced by Grand Valley State University (2000) and Ohio Northern University (2006). She has twice participated in The Public Theater's New Work Now! festival, in 2002 and 2003.

Ana Elena Puga (D.F.A. Dramaturgy and Dramatic Criticism – Yale School of Drama) is an Assistant Professor at The Ohio State University, with a joint appointment in the departments of Theatre and Spanish & Portuguese. She has translated plays by Latin American playwrights such as Juan Radrigán, Carlos Manuel Varela, and Griselda Gambaro, among others. Her translation of six Radrigán plays, with Mónica Núñez-Parra, *Finished from the Start and Other Plays*, was published by Northwestern University Press in 2008. Her study of South American theater under dictatorship, *Memory, Allegory, and Testimony in South American Theater: Upstaging Dictatorship*, was published by Routledge in 2008. Her translation of Patricia Suárez's *Matchmaker* was selected for a 2012 mainstage production at OSU.